D1552968

OLD-FASHIONED CANDYMAKING

Antique chocolate molds, English, German, and Columbian; chocolate stirrers, Mexican.

OLD-FASHIONED CANDYMAKING

June Roth

HENRY REGNERY COMPANY
CHICAGO

Library of Congress Cataloging in Publication Data

Roth, June Spienwak.
 Old-fashioned candymaking.

 1. Confectionery. I. Title.
TX791.R84   641.8'53   74-6906
ISBN 0-8092-8892-3

Copyright © 1974 by June Spienwak Roth. All rights reserved.
Published by Henry Regnery Company
114 West Illinois Street, Chicago, Illinois 60610
Manufactured in the United States of America
Library of Congress Catalog Card Number: 74-6906
International Standard Book Number: 0-8092-8892-3

In loving memory of my maternal grandparents,
Kate and Morris Glazer,
and to their family who live and had lived
—but with special nostalgia for my dear Uncle Bill

Contents

Foreword

Perhaps you missed the era of trolley cars, the organ grinder with a monkey dancing to collect a few pennies, the thrill of a wad of spun sugar bought at the traveling circus, milk delivered to the accompaniment of the clip-clop of a horse and wagon on cobblestone streets, or the haunting tunes of the calliope. People seemed to have more fun then. Perhaps they did not have as much money, speed, and success, but they did have a great soup pot on the back of an everwarm coal stove, and a loaf of fresh bread baking within. And they had the ability to create their own good times, despite the lack of telephones, radios, and television sets.

As the people of the seventies remember years gone by, there seems to be a yearning to relive some of those times. One way to do so is to rediscover the simple joy of making old-fashioned candy in your own kitchen. I've tried to make it easy by providing every kind of nostalgic candy recipe you may remember. If something has been missing from the tempo of your life, perhaps you will find it here.

June Roth

Acknowledgments

The author wishes to express special thanks to Best Foods, a Division of C.P.C. International, for providing photographs and information, and these copyrighted Karo ads:

Karo ad, making fudge, page 30

Karo ad, page 82

Deep appreciation also goes to the following companies for permission to reproduce these copyrighted photographs:

Courtesy of American Pop Corn Company:

Jolly Time Ad, page 142

Courtesy of the American Sugar Company:

"The Sweetest Things in Life" ad, page 116

Early Domino ad, page 16

Courtesy of the Chocolate Manufacturers Association of the U.S.A.:

Frontispiece

chocolate finishes, page 25

Chocolate molds, page 27

Courtesy of General Foods Corporation:

La Belle Chocolatiere, page 92

"The Cheater" ad, page 22

"The Wedding Present" ad, page 108

Courtesy of the Hershey Chocolate Corporation:

Electric car, page 94

Hershey labels, page 93

Early Hershey factory, page 95

In addition, the author wishes to express gratitude for valuable information and photographs to: American Sugar Company; California Prune Advisory Board; General Foods Corporation; Hershey Chocolate Company; Knox Gelatine, Inc.; National Confectioners Association; The Nestle Company; the Vermont Development Department; and Sugar Information, Inc.

RECIPES

NEW
DAINTIES
MADE WITH

CRYSTAL
Domino
Granulated
SUGAR

THE AMERICAN SUGAR REFINING COMPANY

Old-Fashioned Fun
in the Kitchen

When was the last time you whipped up a batch of fudge or joined in a taffy pulling spree? There was an era when these activities were highlights of simple living. One way to regain the nostalgic pleasures of earlier years is by learning how to make candy at home. All you need are a few kitchen utensils, several readily available ingredients, and a little know-how. Don't be surprised if you discover an easy and inexpensive way to have an old-fashioned good time!

Aside from being a treat to eat on the spot, candy is also a quick source of energy, which may be stored in tight containers for long periods of time. As you start to make candy successfully at home, you will soon realize that these sweets are an ideal gift to share with others. Wrap them the old-fashioned way—in pretty boxes with paper doilies and colorful ribbons.

The candy that you make probably will be tastier and prettier than the first candies made by the pioneers. They depended mostly on the availability of sugar, one of the more popular com-

1

modities of world trade. Housewives in the Northeast learned how to make candy from maple sugar, adding nuts to it when they were available. The Indians taught settlers how to find flavors in wintergreen berries, peppermint, spearmint, and in the roots of the iris and ginger plants. Settlers learned that the bark of the sassafras tree could lend variety to their limited supply of ingredients. Chocolate and corn syrup were several centuries in coming to the rescue of the first candymakers in America.

It took many generations for homemade candy to become a rarity, replaced by store-bought sweets that eventually became very popular. The Dutch bakers of the colony of New Amsterdam, later called New York, were making sweets for celebrations in the seventeenth century. The first actual candy shop in America was opened in 1712. It wasn't until the middle of the nineteenth century, however, that technology and commerce advanced to enable an industry of mass-produced confections to spring up.

By the end of the 1800s a flourishing business was done in "penny candies." Where simple candies previously had been dispensed in pharmacies and grocery stores, there now appeared a rash of penny candy stores—all with children as steady customers.

In 1911 another candy wave hit the nation—this time it was the manufactured candy bar, an individually wrapped concoction of chocolate, caramel, nuts, and nougats. With the introduction of the candy bar, many of the popular candies were packaged in five- and ten-cent sizes. Manufacturers found that taste preferences varied in different sections of the country. Easterners seemed to prefer dark and semi-sweet chocolate and miniature sizes. Westerners preferred lighter milk chocolates, mainly in jumbo sizes, and Midwesterners, possibly because they were in the middle, shared a taste for some of each. Wintergreen flavor wins favor with New Englanders, while Midwesterners have a liking for the spicier tastes of cinnamon, mint, and nutmeg. Southerners, who are accustomed to the flavor of local fruit, prefer their hard candies in fruit flavors too.

The candy industry today has reached the point where Americans consume an average of nineteen pounds of sweets a year. Most of the manufactured candies have never been touched by human hands. The high price of labor and sanitary considerations have made hand-dipped chocolates and home-style candies a rarity. Fortunately, as the trend of reaching back to the good old days continues, the desire to recreate the era of nostalgic homemade candymaking is growing. It is easier to do at home these days because our forefathers learned how to manufacture some of the basic ingredients that are the backbone of a candy recipe—sugar, maple sugar, corn syrup, and chocolate. These, in combination with natural products such as milk, butter, eggs, grain, fruit, and nuts, are all that are needed for homemade candies. Let's trace the evolution of these basic ingredients as they weave in and out of the history of the world.

THE SUGAR STORY All green plants make sucrose (sugar) in their leaves, but sugarcane and sugar beets supply most of the sugar used commercially. When it is in the form of common household sugar, it is the most important ingredient in making candy. Once an expensive luxury that only the wealthy could afford, it is now a staple in almost every kitchen.

The path of sugar from its natural state to the pantry shelf in many ways is a study of the history of people. Mention is made of "honey bearing reeds" in the Old Testament and in the records of Admiral Nearchus of the expedition of Alexander the Great down the Indus in 325 B.C. In the time of Nero, Dioscorides wrote of a "hard honey" found upon canes in India.

During the seventh century, A.D. China sent ambassadors to India to learn how to extract syrup from sugarcane. The Indians used to boil the syrup down into a liquid that produced a dark brown sugar paste, similar to the dark brown sugar we have today.

In the eighth century, a crude refining process was invented by the Egyptians. The Arabs also brought sugarcane from the Nile Valley to Sicily. Crusaders in the Middle Ages learned about sugar from the Moslems and spread the word as they returned to their homelands in Europe. This helped to start trade between the East and the West. When the trade was in danger of being restricted by an invasion of the Turks in Constantinople, new routes were needed to reach India.

Columbus, who sought one of those routes, brought cuttings of sugarcane to give to the Indians of the New World on his second voyage. It was planted in the Dominican Republic and Haiti, as well as in other Caribbean Islands, where it still flourishes today.

Methods for refining the sugar were still very primitive when a fifteenth-century inventor in Venice devised a technique of molding sugar into cone-shaped loaves, known as "pains de Venise." For his efforts, he collected what was then a fortune, 100,000 crowns, and this process of molding sugar was used until the middle of the nineteenth century.

Sugarcane grows best in warm places such as Cuba, Puerto Rico, India, Java, the Philippines, Hawaii, South America, Egypt, South Africa, Formosa, and Australia. In the United States, it is grown primarily in the state of Louisiana and to a lesser degree in Florida. Sugar beets can be grown in more temperate zones and are a popular crop in many parts of the United States.

The fine white crystals with which we are familiar today are a far cry from the coarse sweet brownish lumps used up until the nineteenth century. Modern scientific methods were needed before people could conceive the idea of extracting the juice from the cane and the sugar beet, and then refining it into clean sweet crystals.

The American Sugar Refining Company has been doing that since 1891. It manufactures three well-known brands—Domino, Franklin, and Sunny Cane. Five large refineries located in Boston, Brooklyn, Philadelphia, Baltimore, and New Orleans turn out about 17 million pounds of pure cane sugar every working day.

It all starts with a type of grass similar to the "honey bearing reeds" mentioned in the Bible. Foot-long pieces of stalks are planted end-to-end in long furrows. "Eyes" in the stalks sprout into new plants, and in some areas, one such planting will produce crops annually for up to ten years.

When the cane is ready to harvest, it is cut close to the ground, stripped of leaves and tops, loaded into carts, trucks, or railroad cars, and taken to a nearby mill. It must be processed quickly, for it deteriorates rapidly.

The canes are washed, shredded, and rolled to extract the precious juice. The juice is then clarified and processed to remove any impurities. Then it is boiled to reduce it to a thick syrup. The syrup is concentrated further in vacuum pans where crystallization eventually takes place. At this point the product is subjected

Molding sugar cones, 17th century.

to centrifugal force to spin off the clinging thin film of molasses that surrounds each crystal. The brownish substance that remains is known as "raw sugar."

Dark and light brown sugars are produced in the process of refining granulated white sugar by permitting a little of the molasses to remain in the sugar. To obtain fine white sugar, the raw product is dissolved again, filtered to remove impurities, and then recrystallized. Finally it is tumbled through a granulator to dry the tiny crystals and then passed through vibrating screens that sort the dry crystals.

According to an old food price list of the times, one pound of sugar sold for a whopping $2.75 in London in 1742. It was a luxury reserved only for the very wealthy. Today the per capita consumption rate in the United States is about thirty pounds for home use every year. Modern technical aspects of refining sugar have made it easy to acquire a generous supply at low cost. "Honey bearing reeds" have come a long way through the centuries to become a common kitchen product in the home.

REFINING CORN SYRUP Corn existed four thousand years ago. This is confirmed by the recent discovery in a Mexican cave of an ear of Indian corn thought to have been grown about 2000 B.C. Temple carvings and pottery produced by the Mayas reveal corn as one of their staple foods. The ancient Aztecs pictured their god Quetzalcoatl with a cooking pot in one hand and a cornstalk in the other.

Along with the cacao beans brought back to Spain by Columbus were several ears of corn, which had also been discovered in the new land. When the early settlers arrived, they were saved from starvation by gifts of corn from the Indians, and they soon learned how to plant it themselves. As pioneers moved westward, they, too, sowed corn, unaware that they were establishing what is now called the "Corn Belt" of the Midwest. Although corn was an old source of food, the knowledge of how to convert it to a sweetener had not yet been discovered.

Actually it was thought that Napoleon inspired the manufacture of sweeteners from starch when he offered a reward of 100,000 francs to anyone who could figure out the way to do it. France's war with England at the time had put a stop to cane sugar imports, making a substitution necessary. A German scientist soon discovered that cooking potato starch with an acid yielded a thick syrup that tasted sweet, while a French chemist found a way to obtain a sweet substance from grapes. Soon other methods were used to convert starch into a sugar substitute, but the research slowed down when the blockade of Europe was lifted in 1814 and cane sugar could be imported again.

Interest in the conversion of starch to sugar rose again in the United States. In 1866 sugar was made from corn in a factory in Buffalo, New York. Records show that as early as 1902, blue label Karo syrup was made and marketed by the Corn Products Company in Peoria, Illinois. About 1910 red label light corn syrup was marketed too. Different colors were used, so stockboys who could not read would be able to separate the light and dark syrups more easily on the grocery shelves.

The Karo trademark may have been a contraction of an older trademark "Kairomel" that was used by the Glucose Sugar Refining Company. Some say it was a new name, coined by Dr. Wagner, chief chemist for the Corn Products Company.

Crushing sugarcane, Arkansas, late 1800s.

The procedures used in 1866 are still in use, although the equipment and techniques have been improved. Basically corn starch is mixed with water and heated in the presence of a catalyst, which converts the starch to dextrose sugar and dextrins. This starch water is then pressure-cooked in a converter tank until it becomes corn syrup. The syrup is filtered and evaporated until a clear sweet liquid emerges. That clear liquid is mixed with refiners' syrup or sugar, vanilla or maple molasses or honey flavoring, and often has caramel coloring added.

Starch sugar, as corn syrup was called in Europe in the Napoleonic Era, was used mainly in the manufacture of liquors and in brewing beers and ales. Today it is widely used. Besides its use in confections, it is also significant in the manufacture of ice cream and other frozen desserts, jams, jellies, and preserves.

When making candy, corn syrup helps to control the natural tendency of sugar to cool into a hard grainy solid. It helps to produce a smooth texture and keeps candies from drying out too quickly. It also adds body and chewiness to caramels, crunchiness to nut brittle, and clarity to hard candies. You'll find it in either light or dark form in many of the recipes used in this book because it is an important candymaking ingredient—it doesn't cause excessive sweetness and it allows the flavor of other foods to come through. It is just what you need to make good candy.

MAPLE SUGARING   Long before the European settlers arrived in America, the Indians knew about the "sweet water" that dripped from the sugar maple trees. This variety of maple tree is a native of North America that grows in a vast belt extending from Missouri, north around the Great Lakes, then down the St. Lawrence Valley and through New England, New York, and as far south as Virginia. But somehow when we think of maple sugar we think of the state of Vermont, perhaps because its natives have actively promoted the purity and production of a fine quality of maple sugar candies and syrups.

Primitive methods were used to collect the sap from the sugar maple trees from the seventeenth to mid-nineteenth centuries. Wooden buckets hung from wooden spouts, tapped into the trees. They collected the slow dripping that starts about March and continues through April in the colder states. Then each bucket had to be emptied into an iron kettle suspended over an open fire in the woods. Eventually rustic shelters, known as "sugar camps," were built in the woods for this stage.

Rudolph Danforth, who directs the Vermont Sugar House Museum in Royalton, Vermont, remembers when his grandfather used to set out early each morning during sugaring time, driving his team of horses deep into the snow-covered woods. He spent the entire day emptying the buckets in his maple grove, boiling the drippings until they had evaporated to a huge bucketful of maple syrup. The bucket was lugged home to grandmother, who spent her entire, unliberated day boiling the syrup until it became a solid maple sugar. Then, of course, she washed the bucket so grandfather could head for the hills again the next day.

It was mostly a hand operation until the 1880s, when metal spouts and buckets were introduced and a flue-type evaporator was invented. Eventually tractors replaced horses and oxen as a means of pulling the tanks of sap from the woods to the sugarhouse, but each bucket still had to be emptied by hand as the gatherer went from tree to tree. Many farmers in the "sugar bush" country still use the early method of collecting sap, although they may own modern evaporators in which to boil the syrup.

Some big producers today have utilized plastic tubing to replace the old tap-and-bucket set-up. The tubes are inserted into

Quetzalcoatl, an ancient Aztec god, often pictured with cooking pot in one hand and stalk of corn in the other.

each tree so the maple sap can flow directly from the connecting trees to a roadside tank and then to a modern version of the old-time sugarhouse. There the sap flows into an evaporator and its maze of compartments carry the boiling substance to a final "draw off" valve.

It boggles the imagination to realize that a tree must be mature enough to be tapped—about forty years old, "a foot through," and about sixty feet tall. About forty gallons of maple sap are needed to produce one gallon of maple syrup, which, in turn, can produce about eight pounds of maple sugar. Since each tree is capable of producing only ten gallons of sap a season, huge forests of sugar maples are needed to keep the industry going.

Many recipes that use maple syrup for candymaking in this book have been popular for several hundred years and are still in use in sugar maple territory today. In March and early April, Vermont sugarmakers welcome visitors who want to watch how maple syrup is collected and manufactured, and to see the old-time equipment in the sugarhouse museums. The experience brings a great appreciation of the ease with which we can purchase maple syrup for daily use. Better roads into the woods, modern equipment, and advanced technology in boiling methods have turned "sweet water" into a thriving industry.

Although cacao beans were brought back to the court of King Ferdinand of Spain by Columbus, the potential of these strange beans was not realized at the time. A short time later, when the explorer Cortez conquered the Aztec Indians in Mexico, he found that Montezuma's followers were drinking a royal drink called "chocolatl." It was very bitter, but the Spaniards found it to be an aristocratic beverage when sweetened with cane sugar.

Spanish royalty managed to keep the use of cacao beans a secret for most of the sixteenth century, while increasing its production by planting cacao in its warm overseas possessions. But who could keep such a good secret forever? As the royalty and monks continued to drink chocolate, some must have been offered to their foreign guests. At any rate, its use was finally spread to other parts of Europe, and by 1728 manufacturing companies for chocolate were developed in England. By 1756 Germany got into the act, with France following in 1760.

Not too surprisingly, the cacao bean had a round-trip ticket across the Atlantic. John Hannon, a poor but skilled chocolate maker from Ireland, started a small factory in Dorchester, Massachusetts in 1765. He was financed by Dr. James Baker, who eventually bought the outstanding interest in the mill when Hannon was lost at sea. The accident occurred when Hannon sailed to the West Indies to purchase cacao beans for his flourishing business. Dr. Baker continued the operations of the chocolate business himself, and was the founder of the first Baker's brand chocolate in 1780. But it was actually when his grandson, Walter Baker, ran the company that the Baker's trademark of the Chocolate Girl label, became famous.

The drawing of Baker's "La Belle Chocolatière" is America's oldest grocery trademark. It is a copy of a portrait by Jean Etienne Liotard, a Swiss portrait painter of the time. The story behind the painting is rather charming, as the subject was a pretty waitress who worked in one of the quaint chocolate shops that were springing up in Vienna in the mid-1700s. She was Anna Beltauf, the daughter of an impoverished knight. In a Cinderella-like story, she served chocolate to a handsome prince who had stopped for refreshments one day. It wasn't too long before Prince Ditrichstein, an Austrian nobleman, married Anna Beltauf and had her portrait done as a wedding gift. But instead of the formal evening gown usually worn for such paintings at the time, she was painted in a Swiss costume serving chocolate. The painting had become famous and had hung in the Dresden Art Gallery in Germany for over a century when it was seen by Henry L. Pierce, then head of the Walter Baker Company. He adapted the famous painting as an appropriate trademark for Baker's Chocolates in 1877. By 1927, after two other family owners had continued to develop the business, it was sold to the General Foods Corporation, who have kept the popular brand name for their excellent line of baking chocolate.

Meanwhile, in Pennsylvania, Milton Hershey was spending years developing a caramel-exporting business. He took a train to the World's Columbian Exposition in Chicago in 1893, and was fascinated by a display of German chocolate-making machinery. He arranged to buy the display and have it shipped to his caramel factory in Lancaster, Pennsylvania, as soon as the fair had ended. Eventually he sold the caramel business and used the profits to develop what he considered to be a more permanent business, that of making chocolate.

He was a forward-thinking man. To help publicize and deliver the chocolate, he bought one of the first "horseless carriages" in 1900. At a breakneck speed of nine miles an hour, the electric-powered automobile was used to attract attention to the up-to-date thinking of the chocolate company. Today an entire town named Hershey exists in Pennsylvania, dedicated to the commercial production of many types of chocolate sold all over the world. You don't need a map to find Hershey—as soon as you are near, you can sniff your way to the center of town.

Chocolate and cocoa are the basic ingredients of many popular homemade candies. They are derived from the cacao bean, primarily grown in portions of Africa, South America, and the Dominican Republic. Methods had to be developed to separate the cacao bean from its shell before processing it into chocolate. First the beans are cleaned, and then roasted to develop the flavor. The roasting also loosens the shell, so the solid chocolate inside the lima-like bean can be processed further. The shells are "air blown" away from the heavier chocolate "nibs" by a step known as "cracking and fanning." The chocolate nibs are further processed into chocolate for eating and cooking as well as other by-products.

The nibs are crushed at a high temperature to liquefy the fat or "cocoa butter." This results in a "chocolate liquor" that is unsweetened baking chocolate when solidified. It is used to process sweet chocolate and milk chocolate or it may be sold without any other addition as unsweetened or "bitter" chocolate.

Cocoa is chocolate liquor from which a portion of the cocoa butter has been removed. Sweet chocolate is a homogeneous mixture of chocolate liquor, extra cocoa butter, sugar, and flavorings. Dried milk is added to make milk chocolate.

To add these ingredients and develop flavor while maintaining a smooth mixture, the chocolate is kneaded in huge conching machines. These are equipped with heavy rollers that plow back and forth through the chocolate mass. The chocolate is then cooled and sold in its liquid form as flavoring, or molded into bars to be distributed as candy or a cooking ingredient.

Lucky us, to be able to reach for an ounce or so of chocolate whenever we are ready to use its flavor in making candy.

Basic Equipment
for Candymaking

A heavy deep pot and a long, wooden spoon technically are all you need to get started making candy. But it is difficult to work without a good candy thermometer, and it is helpful to have a marble slab. When you have discovered how easy and creative candymaking can be, you may want to acquire a few other tools to help you cope with several of the more complicated procedures in a comfortable way.

Any old pot won't do for cooking candy. If it is thin and flimsy, the mixture will burn. If it is shallow, the mixture might foam up over the top—making a sticky mess to clean up afterwards. If it has too large a top surface in proportion to its height, the mixture will evaporate too fast. The best choice then would be a heavy, deep, straight-sided pot with a rounded bottom—something made of iron, copper, or very heavy aluminum. To prevent the ingredients from boiling over, select a pot that seems to be too large for the ingredients involved—and remember to grease the top inch of the inside rim.

13

A regular double boiler will be used over and over again in chocolate candymaking. If necessary, substitute a heavy saucepan sitting in another pan filled with several inches of water. If you try to skip the layer of simmering water, you are liable to scorch the candy.

For peanut brittles and several other types of candy that call for the use of a heavy skillet, the old, black cast-iron type is best, but any heavy, large skillet will work. Often the new light-weight cooking utensils do not retain the heat and prevent burning at the same time. They are easy on the wrist when lifting, but they are really only meant for fast-cooking procedures.

An ordinary flour sifter is just the thing for reducing confectioners' sugar to dust or breaking up the lumps in cocoa. Never wash a sifter—just work all the contents out and wipe it clean.

A long, wooden spoon is best for stirring the hot mixture. Also useful is a flat, wooden paddle made especially for this purpose or a disposable, flat stick that is used to mix paint. There is so much stirring involved that a metal spoon might scratch the pot and certainly will retain too much heat for comfort.

The most important investment is a well-constructed candy thermometer. It is helpful because cooking sugar is a technical operation that requires careful testing as you go, and a thermometer is the most accurate way to test. Many homemade candy experts insist that both the thermometer and the water testing methods (discussed in detail in the next chapter) must be used for best results. Certainly you must use one or the other of the gauging techniques to know when to stop the heat and finish off the confection. The two most common problems with homemade candy are starting to beat the candy too soon, and not beating it long enough. Testing tells you exactly when to stop the heat; following the recipe directions carefully will help to prevent underbeating.

Certain recipes call for a spatula wrapped in layers of wet cheesecloth to wipe away sugar crystals that may form around the inside rim of the pot. A clean pastry brush or a new sponge may be used instead.

If you are planning to make fondant, you will need a 3½-inch, broad, steel-bladed spatula that will not bend easily. If you can't find one in a housewares store, try to find a suitable steel implement in a hardware store. Rub the sharp edges of a new steel spatula with sandpaper or an emery cloth to prevent scratching the surface on which you use it.

Accurate measuring cups and spoons are essential too, if you want uniform quality for your efforts. Don't rely on guesswork by using an old teacup or a standard teaspoon—¼, ½, and ¾ cannot be measured exactly even by a practiced eye.

If there is no strong arm handy for beating the mixture, consider using a portable electric mixer for this chore. Some are toys and some can do a heavy-duty job, so test the action of any mixer before you make the purchase.

You will also need a variety of baking sheets and rimmed pans. Large platters will also be of great use when a marble slab is not available. A professional caramel cutter that makes thirty uniform squares at a time, is useful, but it is not necessary as long as you have several sizes of sharpened knives.

Another professional piece of equipment is a funnel-and-stick, used to regulate the size of poured mints and molded candies. This may be purchased in a restaurant supply store that handles confectioners' equipment.

A professional chocolate dipping fork and a cherry dipping fork are also useful, if you intend to venture into these areas of candymaking. A two-tined fork, such as a fish or fondue fork, may be substituted for either of these until you know whether you want to repeat the performance.

Lollipop sticks, jelly apple sticks, tiny crinkled paper cups, waxed paper, aluminum foil, and plastic wrap are all optional necessities, depending on what is called for in the recipe. Heavy-duty, freezer wrapping paper is a fine product to use when greased waxed paper is required.

Many people wear gloves when handling warm taffy. Use plain cotton or leather gloves for this, rather than anything fuzzy that will stick to the candy.

Lastly, have a small container of warm water near the range so you can deposit the stirring paddle, candy thermometer, and pastry brush or spatula into it as they are taken out of the hot mixture. Swish them around to remove all sugar crystals if you need to use them again.

Cooking Sugar into Candy

Although each recipe has specific directions designed to produce perfect homemade candy, it is important to understand the playfulness of sugar as it cooks through stages of intensifying heat. Each stage can be identified by the degrees on a candy thermometer, and also by what is known as the "cold water test."

The simplest way to describe the temperatures of candymaking is to think of an elevator. Before you get on, you have to know where to step off. And so it is with cooking sugar—as the temperature climbs on the thermometer, you have to know exactly when to remove the pot from the heat to stop the cooking action. As with the elevator, if you don't get off in time, you'll be on the next level before you can do anything about it. And the stages of cooking sugar only go one way—up.

The best kind of candy thermometer is paddle shaped, with a clip that fits over the side of the saucepan, permitting the bulb to be completely covered with the cooking syrup without touching the bottom of the pan. Try to find a gauge that has each candy stage plainly printed next to the calibrations.

Sea level sometimes makes a difference in the temperature, so to be on the safe side in high altitude areas, bring a pan of water to a full boil and note how many degrees under the normal 212°F. (sea level boiling point) the thermometer registers. Roughly, the temperature is 2°F. less for every 1,000 feet above sea level. When preparing candy in a place that is 3,000 feet above sea level, the thermometer will show a boiling point of 6°F. less than the normal 212°F.—or 206°F. This means that in all recipes, 6°F. should be deducted from the stated degrees. For example, if a recipe calls for 250°F., aim for 244°F. instead.

Weather affects candy cooking in subtle ways. It is best to choose a cool, dry day, as dampness and humidity also may cause changes in the degrees required. A general rule of thumb is to add 2° to the target degrees on a damp, humid day. If a recipe calls for 250°F., aim for 252°F. instead.

For greatest accuracy when either altitude or humidity is a factor, try to use a candy thermometer and a "cold water test." The cold water test brings two of your sharpest senses into play— sight and touch. It is based on the fact that a small amount of the hot candy mixture dropped into a bowl of cold water will react in different ways according to its temperature and cooking stage.

This is what to look and feel for:

232° to 234°F.—Thread or very soft ball stage. When a small amount of syrup is dropped from a spoon into cold water, it will spin a thin thread and it can be molded together with the fingers to form a ball that falls apart when lifted out of the water. This is the level to remove the candy mixture from the heat to make syrups and frostings.

234° to 240°F.—Soft ball stage. When a small amount of syrup is dropped from a spoon into cold water, it will form a ball that holds together but flattens slightly when removed from the water. This is the level to remove the candy mixture from the heat to make fondant or fudge.

244° to 248°F.—Firm ball stage. When a small amount of syrup is dropped from a spoon into cold water, it will form a firm ball that retains its shape when lifted out of the water. This is the level to remove the candy mixture from the heat to make caramels.

250° to 266°F.—Hard ball stage. When a small amount of syrup is dropped from a spoon into cold water, it will form a ball of candy that is compact and hard enough when removed from the water to make a sound when tapped against the side of a dish. This is the level to remove the candy mixture from the heat to make divinity and taffy.

270° to 285°F.—Soft crack stage. When a small amount of syrup is dropped from a spoon into cold water, it will separate into hard but not brittle threads. This is the level to remove the candy mixture from the heat to make toffee and jelly apples.

290° to 310°F.—Hard crack stage. When a small amount of syrup is dropped from a spoon into cold water, it will separate into brittle threads that break easily when removed from the water. This is the level to remove the candy mixture saucepan from the heat to make brittles and hard candies.

When the temperature is permitted to rise above 310°F., the syrup begins to change color, at first taking on a light caramel hue and later changing to a dark brown. Over 350°F. the syrup will have a decidedly burnt taste and become useless for any kind of candymaking. It will seem as though the temperature takes its own sweet time to climb up the thermometer, but don't be lulled into a false sense of security. The pace changes after 220°F., suddenly rising faster and faster.

With such changing activity going on during the cooking of candy, it makes good sense to read the recipe through before you start. Assemble all the ingredients you will need and have your measuring cups and spoons and other utensils nearby.

Be sure that you have prepared the proper receptacle for the hot syrup when it is removed from the heat, because that's when you will have to work fast, following the remaining directions to create the variation of candy you have chosen.

When you are ready to start, clip the thermometer on the side of a saucepan and leave it there during the entire cooking time. Stir the mixture continuously until the sugar is dissolved, and then abstain from stirring at all so you do not cause crystallization to occur. If sugar crystals form on the inside of the saucepan, wipe the area immediately with either dampened cheesecloth wrapped around a spatula or even a fork, or use a wet pastry brush or a small new paint brush. Rinse the crystals off at once in the container of warm water you have set near the range. Keep the heat steady and hot when cooking non-stir candies, cooking them as fast and as evenly as possible.

Whenever a recipe contains butter, cream, milk, chocolate, or molasses, the "hands off, do not stir" policy is revoked. These ingredients cause candy to boil very high (and these are the candies that need the over-sized pots) and to burn if not stirred continuously. Stir, stir, stir to avoid a messy spillover and a burnt batch of candy.

Extracts should be used drop by drop to produce a delicately flavored confection. Use only the best grade and use it sparingly because a little goes a long way. The same advice goes for vegetable coloring that is used to tint the syrup into appetizing shades.

Use a pastry brush and a tasteless salad oil to coat pans and the marble slab, if directed to do so in the recipe. Margarine may be used interchangeably with butter for this purpose as well, and for buttering your hands for pulling taffy, but if large amounts of butter are listed for a recipe it is better not to make the substitution.

Once you have learned to test each stage of cooking sugar, and whether or not to stir as the ingredients themselves demand, you will be well on your way to making fine, reliable candy.

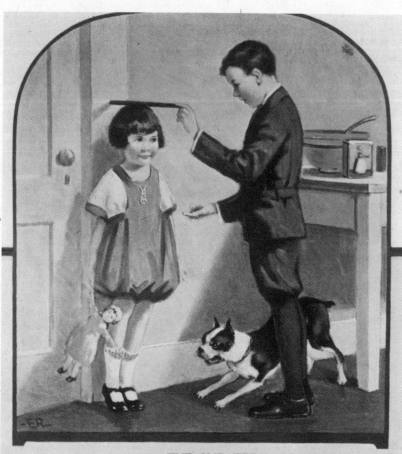

"THE CHEATER"

Nowadays when so much attention is paid to the development and nutrition of children it is well to remember that

Baker's Breakfast Cocoa

is a genuine food drink, pure and delicious. It contains a much larger proportion of cocoa butter than is found in inferior grades.

Measures up to all the standards

Made only by

WALTER BAKER & CO. LTD.

Established 1780 DORCHESTER, MASS.

Canadian Mills at Montreal

Old advertisement for Baker's Chocolate.

Hand-Dipping and Molding Chocolates

There is an art to tempering chocolate. Tempering is the act of working the chocolate to reduce it from the melting temperature of 110°F. to the proper dipping temperature of 87°F. Just cooling it is not enough—it must be manipulated, aerated, and cooled all at once. Although the technique is complicated when producing great quantities for a commercial venture, it is relatively easy to learn how to make small batches of marvelous chocolates.

First, you must buy several pounds of pure milk chocolate, semi-sweet or bitter, depending on your preference. This may be difficult to obtain, but a local confectioner may be willing to sell less than the usual ten-pound slab. (Some suppliers, however, will not fill less than a fifty-pound order.) For small quantities, use the packaged pure chocolate that is available at some food markets. Read the label carefully, as it should not be baking chocolate, but rather, coating chocolate, which already contains cocoa butter and sugar.

Use a double boiler to melt the chocolate, remembering never to let the water that is in the lower saucepan actually come to a boil, but rather keep it at a simmer until the chocolate is just melted. Break the bars into pieces so they will melt faster. The nice thing about working with chocolate, is that it can be kept warm in the top of the double boiler. Even the leftovers that have solidified can be scraped and remelted in the warming chocolate.

Chocolate melts at a temperature range of 110° to 120°F. Try to work next to the melting chocolate for greatest efficiency, even if you have to plug in an electric hotplate or warming tray near the candymaking area. With a paint scraper, scoop out several spatula loads of melted chocolate onto a marble slab or a low-rimmed jelly-roll pan. Quickly work the chocolate back and forth, over and under, keeping it in a constant small pool on the working surface.

After a few minutes, pick up a dab of the chocolate with an index finger and tap it lightly into the indentation under your lower lip—if it feels warm, keep on working the chocolate and re-test every minute. Body temperature is usually at 98.6°F., so when you feel a sudden cold shock in the space above your chin, it means the chocolate has reduced to a temperature between 87° and 90°F. The chocolate has been properly tempered. It is an easy process if you paddle only two or three spatulafuls at a time.

The whole process of tempering a small amount of chocolate takes from three to five minutes, and it is the most important step in working with chocolate so do not cheat on the testing. If it is not the right temperature, the candy will be dull and there may even be whitish streaks in the finished product. If it gets too cool, of course, it will solidify and you will have to scoop it up, return to the melting pot, and start all over again. A marble slab helps because it is always 11°F. less than room temperature and will cool candy quickly.

Add flavoring oil, if needed, a few moments before the chocolate is tempered. Orange, peppermint, or coffee flavoring, administered a few drops at a time, can develop into a taste sensation when the candy hardens.

To hand-dip chocolates, have a tray of fillings close by before the tempering begins. These can include fresh strawberries, nuts, caramels, balls of fondant, and the ever-popular maraschino

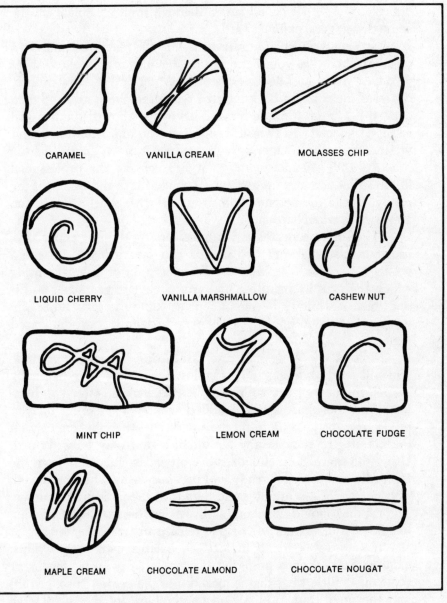

CARAMEL   VANILLA CREAM   MOLASSES CHIP

LIQUID CHERRY   VANILLA MARSHMALLOW   CASHEW NUT

MINT CHIP   LEMON CREAM   CHOCOLATE FUDGE

MAPLE CREAM   CHOCOLATE ALMOND   CHOCOLATE NOUGAT

The swirls on top of hand-dipped chocolate indicate its interior contents.

cherries. When the chocolate is ready for dipping, pick up the filling with an index and third finger. Slosh it quickly into the chocolate and coat on all sides. Remove from chocolate on the same two fingers, palm upwards.

Let excess chocolate drain back into the tempered pool for a moment, then turn your hand upside down over a prepared sheet of waxed paper and deposit the dipped piece on it. Now quickly dip your index finger back into the tempered chocolate, and then over the top of the candy you have just dipped—taking just enough chocolate to swirl a design into the top. Lift your finger up and off, as any lingering will produce a messy finish. A little practice and you may want to try to achieve the professional finishes that actually inform the eater what is in the center of the candy. But in the beginning, a circular double swirl makes a fine appearance when hardened.

If you have acquired a two-tined fork for dipping chocolates, use it in place of your two fingers and save a lot of mess and waste. Of course, you will lose the sensation of finger painting which the squishy handling of warm chocolate produces, and it does take a while to become adept at using the fork, especially when you have to flip the candy over to deposit it on the waxed paper.

Molded chocolates are also fascinating to make. For these you will need plastic or rubber molds. These may be individually shaped molds or trays with many small cavities. After you have tempered the chocolate and added whatever flavoring oil you prefer, use the spatula to fill the mold. Tap the mold smartly on the counter to remove any air bubbles that may have formed. Using the spatula, carefully remove all excess chocolate from the top of the mold so the candy will pop out easily when hardened. Refrigerate for ten minutes and then turn the mold upside down. The candies should come out easily. A few taps with the wooden handle of your spatula will help to release any reluctant ones.

It is possible to fill molded chocolates with cashew nuts, candied fruit (already prepared and available as for fruitcake), or some other little treat that is tucked into the center. If so, just fill half the mold, tap to eliminate air bubbles, let the mold set a moment after you have tipped it to coat all sides of the mold. Then turn the mold upside down over the pool of chocolate and

Two methods of using chocolate molds.

let the excess drip off. Refrigerate for 4 minutes. Fill each center with whatever you have decided upon, then fill in all the gaps with additional tempered chocolate, smooth off the top and remove excess chocolate as you did for the plain molded chocolates. Return to the refrigerator for 6 minutes more, then tap out of the mold and store in a covered container. When you see how lovely these candies are, you may want to purchase some crinkled paper cups from a supplier or your local confectioner. They add a professional finishing touch to candies you may want to give as gifts.

The techniques used to make other large molded chocolate figures such as Easter bunnies, are similar to those for using small molds. Large plastic molds usually are available from a professional supplier, but you may have to ask around until you can locate a source. Antique dealers sometimes have the old metal molds, but they are becoming expensive and scarce and are not as easy or sanitary as the plastic ones. To use the large molds, temper a larger pool of chocolate. Fill the mold halfway. Tap to remove air bubbles. Tilt this way and that, so the sides are well coated. Set on the counter for several moments. Pour off excess chocolate from the mold, if you wish to make it hollow. Otherwise fill the mold completely. Trim excess chocolate from the edges so it will slip out easily. (You can store the excess chocolate, and use it later.) Clamp shut. Refrigerate for 10 minutes for a solid mold and 15 minutes for a hollow one. Slip off clamps and slide out the chocolate figure. Wrap it in cellophane or plastic wrapping.

Chocolate left in the melting pot and excess scrapings from your work area may be stored at a cool temperature until you are ready to work again. All chocolate should be stored in a cool, dry place, with a temperature of no more than 78°F. When the temperature is higher, the cocoa butter in chocolate softens and rises to the surface, where it forms a gray film known as "bloom." This is safe to eat, but it may not taste as creamy or look as attractive. Solid chocolate with "bloom" may be melted down or used for baking.

Sweet and semi-sweet chocolates may develop "sugar bloom" if stored in very moist atmospheres. This is a rough grayish layer that results from solution and recrystallization of sugar in the chocolate. Chocolate with "sugar bloom" may be used for cooking or baking.

Milk chocolate in particular will absorb flavors and odors of other foods, and so it must be wrapped very tightly to remain fresh tasting.

Chocolate may be refrigerated, but it becomes very brittle if you do so. It may be frozen for as long as 3 or 4 months without a change in flavor, texture, or appearance.

Master the art of tempering chocolate and you'll be well on your way to fun or profit. You will also be producing chocolate with no preservatives, no artificial additives, and of the type that sells for many dollars per pound in specialty shops.

Fudge, Penuche, and Patience

There was a time when a young lady could count on a treasured recipe for sweet and creamy fudge to bring her popularity. Understandably she would be reluctant to part with such a recipe that filled her parlor with sweet-toothed swains. And it was not only traditional chocolate fudge that made good bait, but all sorts of flavors and variations—including penuche and patience candies.

This chapter is chock-full of such heirloom recipes and many new ideas as well. But it's important to beware of the two major pitfalls of making fudge, so you don't produce a panful of dull and grainy goo. First, be sure to follow directions on cooling the mixture before beating it, and then be sure to beat it enough to give it a creamy texture.

Unless directed otherwise, stir only until the sugar is completely dissolved. Cook without stirring, even if the temptation to mix a little seems irresistible—stirring at the wrong time can cause the sugar to crystallize.

When a pan is removed from the heat, try not to disturb the ingredients. Use the least amount of motion—just set the mixture aside and let it cool. An electric beater is a great asset in insuring that a mixture is beaten long enough. When done by hand, beat with hard definite strokes and keep the action steady.

Then pour the fudge and let it set. Don't cut until the fudge is firm and cold, although the surface may be marked into squares when warm. These precautions will give you a delicious batch of fudge every time.

Once you have mastered the art of fudge-making, you will want to try the two-flavored rolls and other variations. Many fudges have unusual ingredients—one is even made with left-over mashed potatoes. When directions give a boiling time, rather than a degree to reach on the candy thermometer, watch the clock carefully to avoid overcooking.

The nice thing about fudge is that it can be prepared in just a short time, as most recipes are cooked only to the soft ball stage. It cools rather quickly too, so you'll be cutting squares and passing the platter within an hour.

SIMPLE CHOCOLATE FUDGE

4 squares unsweetened chocolate, 1-ounce size
1½ cups milk
4 cups sugar
⅛ teaspoon salt
¼ cup butter
2 teaspoons vanilla

Butter an 8-inch square pan. Place chocolate and milk in a heavy saucepan. Cook and stir over very low heat until mixture is smooth, well blended, and slightly thickened. Add sugar and salt; stir over medium heat until sugar is dissolved and mixture boils. Continue boiling over medium heat, without stirring, until small amount of mixture forms a soft ball that can be rolled with the fingers into a definite shape in cold water—a temperature of 234°F. on the candy thermometer. Remove from heat; add butter and vanilla. Do not stir. Cool to lukewarm, 110°F. Then beat until mixture begins to lose its gloss and holds its shape. Pour at once into pan. Cool until set; then cut into squares. Let stand in pan until firm. Makes about 36 pieces.

CHOCOLATE BAR FUDGE

1 milk chocolate bar, 7-ounce size, broken into squares
1 dark sweet chocolate bar, 7-ounce size, broken into squares
1 cup marshmallow crème
1 tablespoon butter
1 teaspoon vanilla
2 cups sugar
1 cup evaporated milk
1 cup chopped nuts

Butter a 9-inch square pan. Combine chocolate bar pieces, marshmallow creme, butter and vanilla in a 3-quart saucepan; set aside. In another 3-quart saucepan, combine sugar and milk; heat, stirring constantly, until mixture boils. Continue to stir and boil for 6 minutes. Pour sugar mixture over chocolate mixture in saucepan; blend well. Stir in nuts. Pour into the pan; chill several hours. Cut in squares. Makes about 36 pieces.

SMOOTH CHOCOLATE FUDGE

¼ cup butter
3 ounces unsweetened chocolate
1 pound confectioners' sugar
⅓ cup instant, nonfat dry milk
½ cup light or dark corn syrup
1 tablespoon water
1 teaspoon vanilla
½ cup chopped nuts

Butter an 8-inch square pan. Melt butter and chocolate in top of a 2-quart double boiler or saucepan over boiling water. Meanwhile, sift confectioners' sugar and nonfat dry milk together; set aside. Stir corn syrup, water, and vanilla into chocolate mixture over boiling water. Blend in sifted dry ingredients, one-half at a time, stirring each time until mixture is well blended and smooth. Remove from boiling water. Mix in nuts. Turn into the pan. Cool. Cut into squares. Makes about 36 pieces.

NOTE: If necessary, fudge may be prepared over low direct heat. Stir constantly while butter and chocolate are melting. Dry ingredients may be unsifted if desired, but extra caution is necessary to insure a smooth result.

Smooth chocolate fudge.

BLONDE FUDGE

¼ cup butter
1 pound confectioners' sugar
⅓ cup instant, nonfat dry milk
½ cup light corn syrup
1 tablespoon water
2 teaspoons vanilla

Butter an 8-inch square pan. Melt butter in the top of a double boiler over hot water. Meanwhile, sift confectioners' sugar and nonfat dry milk together; set aside. Stir corn syrup, water and vanilla into butter, over boiling water. Blend in sifted dry ingredients, one-half at a time, stirring each time until mixture is well blended and smooth. Remove from heat and turn into the pan. Cool. Cut into squares. Makes about 36 pieces.

FUDGE ROLL

2 cups chopped nuts
1 batch SMOOTH CHOCOLATE FUDGE
1 batch BLONDE FUDGE

Butter two 9-inch square pans; cover the bottom of one pan with the chopped nuts. Prepare Smooth Chocolate Fudge as directed. Pour over the nuts; spread and smooth. Prepare Blonde Fudge as directed and turn into the second greased pan. Let it stand until set, but not too soft. Turn out the chocolate fudge onto waxed paper, then turn it over so the nuts are on the bottom. Roll blonde fudge into a tight log and place on one end of the chocolate fudge. Roll chocolate fudge jelly roll fashion around the roll of blonde fudge, using waxed paper as an aid. Chill until firm. Slice with a sharp knife. Makes about 72 pieces of candy.

NOTE: For two rolls, cut each kind of fudge down the middle before assembling. Then roll as directed above, making two slender rolls instead of one large one.

DOUBLE FUDGE

2 cups sugar
½ cup heavy cream
2 squares baking chocolate
2 tablespoons butter
2 cups brown sugar
½ cup heavy cream
1 teaspoon vanilla
1 cup chopped walnuts

Butter a 9-inch square pan. Combine sugar, ½ cup cream, chocolate, and 1 tablespoon butter in a saucepan. Boil for 7 minutes, then beat until creamy. Spread in a pan to cool. Meanwhile, combine brown sugar, ½ cup heavy cream, vanilla, nuts, and remaining butter in a saucepan; boil for 10 minutes, then beat until creamy and pour over first layer of fudge already in the pan. Cool. Cut in squares and serve. Makes about 36 pieces.

REFRIGERATOR FUDGE

2¼ *cups sugar*
¾ *cup undiluted evaporated milk*
2 *packages 6-ounce size semi-sweet chocolate chips*
⅓ *cup corn syrup*
2 *tablespoons butter*
1 *teaspoon vanilla*
1 *cup chopped nuts or raisins (optional)*

Butter an 8-inch square pan. Combine sugar and evaporated milk in a heavy saucepan. Bring to a boil over medium heat, stirring constantly. Reduce heat to low; cook mixture 10 minutes, stirring constantly. Remove from heat. Immediately add chocolate chips, corn syrup, butter, and vanilla. Stir until chocolate is melted and fudge is smooth and creamy. Add nuts or raisins. Stir just until mixed. Pour immediately into the pan. Spread quickly with spatula to give rippled, uneven, shiny top. (Surface will set quickly.) Chill until firm, 1 to 2 hours. Cut into squares. Makes about 36 pieces.

CHOCOLATE-COATED
WHITE OPERA FUDGE

4 *cups sugar*
1⅓ *cups light cream*
¼ *cup light corn syrup*
½ *teaspoon salt*
¼ *cup butter*
2 *teaspoons vanilla*
½ *cup semi-sweet chocolate chips*
5 *squares baking chocolate, 1-ounce size*

Line a baking sheet with waxed paper. Combine sugar, cream, corn syrup, and salt in a heavy 4-quart saucepan. Cook over medium heat, stirring constantly, until mixture boils. Cover and boil gently about 3 minutes. Uncover; cook without stirring to 236°F. on the candy thermometer (soft ball stage). If stirring is necessary toward the end of the cooking, stir gently and avoid splashing. Remove from heat; add butter. Cool to 110°F. and do not stir. Add vanilla and beat candy by hand or with a portable electric mixer until it becomes thick, dull, and light in color. Quickly pour into a buttered 9-inch square pan; cut in small squares, and roll each square into a small ball with a flat bottom. Place the balls on the baking sheet. Cover lightly and chill for 3 to 4 hours, or overnight for best results. These will become the "centers" when they are dipped in chocolate coating.

To make the chocolate coating, cut 6 of the chocolate chips into very small pieces; set aside. Break the baking chocolate into pieces and place in a 1½ cup wide-mouth jar, or a 2-cup glass measuring cup. Add remaining chocolate chips to the baking chocolate. Place jar or measuring cup in a pan of warm water. Water should cover the bottom half of the container. (If any water is allowed to mix with chocolate, the chocolate will thicken and cannot be used for coating.) Keep pan over low heat, but do not allow water temperature to exceed 125°F. When the chocolate starts to melt, stir constantly, until the chocolate is completely melted and blended. Remove jar from water and continue to stir until chocolate is cooled to 88°F. (The container should feel slightly warm to the touch.) Stir shaved chocolate chips into the melted chocolate until completely blended. This is a vital part of the procedure and cannot be omitted. The unmelted chocolate seeds the chocolate coating.

Dip the chilled centers with a hat pin or fondue fork completely into the chocolate, one at a time. Keep chocolate between 84°F. and 86°F. while dipping by placing the container in warm water. Gently tap the hat pin or fork on side of container to remove excess chocolate. Place each candy on waxed paper. Decorate the top of each immediately with a swirl of melted coating, using the tip of the hat pin or fork. Return candy to refrigerator; store in a covered container in refrigerator or cool place. Makes about 36 pieces.

COCOA FUDGE

⅔ cup cocoa
3 cups sugar
⅛ teaspoon salt
1½ cups milk
¼ cup butter
1 teaspoon vanilla

Lightly butter an 8-inch square pan. Thoroughly combine cocoa, sugar, and salt in a 4-quart saucepan; gradually add milk. Bring to a boil over medium heat, stirring constantly. Continue to boil, without stirring, to 234°F. or until a small amount of mixture forms a soft ball when dropped in cold water. Remove saucepan from heat; add butter and vanilla. Do not stir. Cool at room temperature to 110°F. Beat by hand until fudge thickens and loses some of its gloss. Quickly spread fudge in the pan. Cool. Makes about 36 pieces.

COCOA MARSHMALLOW-NUT FUDGE

¾ cup cocoa
3 cups sugar
⅛ teaspoon salt
1½ cups milk
¼ cup butter
1 teaspoon vanilla
1 cup marshmallow crème
1 cup broken nuts

Butter an 8-inch square pan. Thoroughly combine cocoa, sugar, and salt in a 4-quart saucepan; gradually add milk. Bring to a boil on medium heat, stirring constantly. Continue to boil, without stirring, to 234°F. on the candy thermometer (soft ball stage). Remove saucepan from heat; add butter, vanilla, and marshmallow crème. Cool at room temperature to 110°F. without stirring. Then beat vigorously for about 10 minutes, or until fudge thickens and loses some of its gloss. Stir in broken nuts and pour into the pan. Cool and cut in squares. Makes about 36 pieces.

NUT-MARSHMALLOW FUDGE

1⅔ cups evaporated milk
2 cups sugar
2 cups semi-sweet chocolate chips
1 cup coarsely chopped nuts
1 cup miniature marshmallows

Line an 8-inch square pan with 2 strips of waxed paper, leaving a 2-inch overhang on each side. Combine evaporated milk and sugar in a 3-quart saucepan. Place over moderate heat and bring to a full rolling boil, stirring constantly (takes about 4 minutes). Then boil for 5 minutes, stirring constantly. Remove from heat; add chocolate chips and stir until smooth. Fold in chopped nuts and marshmallows. Turn into prepared pan. Chill. Makes about 36 pieces.

COFFEE FUDGE

2 cups sugar
1 cup strong coffee
1 teaspoon heavy cream
1 cup chopped nuts

Butter an 8-inch square pan. Combine sugar, coffee, and cream in a saucepan. Boil for about 8 minutes, until thermometer reaches 234°F. (soft ball stage). Add chopped nuts and beat until creamy. Pour into the pan. Cool. Cut into squares. Makes 16 two-inch pieces of candy.

PEANUT BUTTER FUDGE

¼ cup butter
⅓ cup chunk-style peanut butter
1 pound confectioners' sugar
⅓ cup instant, nonfat dry milk
½ cup light corn syrup
1 tablespoon water
1 teaspoon vanilla

Butter an 8-inch square pan. Melt butter and peanut butter in top of a 2-quart double boiler over boiling water. Meanwhile, sift confectioners' sugar and nonfat dry milk together; set aside. Stir corn syrup, water, and vanilla into peanut butter mixture. Stir in half of the sifted dry ingredients at a time, stirring until mixture is well blended. Remove from boiling water. Turn into the pan. Cool. Cut into squares. Makes about 36 pieces.

From top left, peanut butter fudge; top right, Rocky Road candy; center stuffed dried fruit; center bottom, fudge roll; and bottom left, refrigerator fudge

BUTTERSCOTCH PEANUT FUDGE

2¼ *cups firmly packed light brown sugar*
1 *cup granulated sugar*
½ *cup butter*
1 *cup evaporated milk*
2 *cups butterscotch-flavored chips*
1 *jar marshmallow crème, 7½ to 10-ounce size*
1 *cup chopped peanuts*
½ *cup golden raisins*
1 *teaspoon rum extract*
½ *teaspoon vanilla*

Butter two 8-inch square pans. In a 2½-quart saucepan, combine brown and white sugars, butter, and milk. Place over medium heat and stir until butter is melted. Cook over medium heat, stirring occasionally, until mixture reaches 238°F. on the candy thermometer (soft ball stage). Remove from heat; stir in butterscotch-flavored chips and marshmallow cream until thoroughly blended. Add peanuts, golden raisins, rum extract, and vanilla. Pour into the pans. When cold, cut into squares. The candy may be kept in a closed container. Makes about 72 pieces.

GRAHAM CRACKER FUDGE

2 cups sugar
2 squares unsweetened chocolate, 1-ounce size
1 cup cream
1 pound small marshmallows
2 cups crushed graham crackers
1 cup chopped nuts
2 tablespoons butter
1 teaspoon vanilla

Butter two 8-inch square pans. Combine sugar, chocolate, and cream in a large saucepan. Cook over medium heat, stirring constantly, until mixture begins to boil. Then cook without stirring, keeping heat just high enough to prevent mixture from boiling over. (Wash down sides of saucepan occasionally with a pastry brush dipped in hot water to prevent crystals from forming.) Cook to 236° on the candy thermometer (soft ball stage). Then add marshmallows, graham cracker crumbs, nuts, butter, and vanilla; mix well. Pour at once into the pans. Cut into pieces when cool. Makes about 72 pieces.

CHERRY FUDGE

2 cups sugar
1 cup milk
1 tablespoon butter
¼ pound chopped cherries

Butter an 8-inch square pan. Combine sugar, milk, and butter in a saucepan; boil for 8 minutes. Beat until creamy. Add chopped cherries. Pour into the pan. Cool. Cut in squares. Makes about 36 pieces.

FRUITED FUDGE

1⅓ cups evaporated milk
2 cups sugar
2 cups semi-sweet chocolate chips
2½ cups mixed candied fruit

Line an 8-inch square pan with 2 strips of waxed paper, leaving a 2-inch overhang on each side. Combine evaporated milk and sugar in a 3-quart saucepan. Place over moderate heat and bring to a full rolling boil, stirring constantly (about 4 minutes). Then boil for 5 minutes, stirring constantly. Remove from heat; add chocolate chips and stir until smooth. Fold in candied fruit. Turn into prepared pan. Chill. Makes 36 pieces.

ALMOND BARK

3 cups sugar
½ teaspoon salt
1 cup light cream
½ cup milk
¼ cup light corn syrup
2 tablespoons butter
2 teaspoons vanilla
1 can almonds, 6-ounce size

Butter a 15½ by 10½-inch jelly roll pan. Combine sugar, salt, cream, milk, corn syrup, and butter in a heavy 3-quart saucepan. Cook over medium heat, stirring constantly, until sugar is dissolved and mixture boils. Continue cooking, stirring occasionally, until temperature reaches 238°F. on the candy thermometer (soft ball stage). Remove from heat. Stir in vanilla. Cool without stirring, until temperature reaches lukewarm (110°F.), then beat until fudge begins to thicken and loses its gloss. Fold in nuts. Immediately spread into the pan. Cool. Cut into squares when cold. Makes about 36 pieces.

SOUR CREAM FUDGE

2 cups sugar
½ cup dairy sour cream
¼ cup light corn syrup
¼ cup butter
2 tablespoons cocoa
1 teaspoon vanilla
1 cup chopped nuts

Butter an 8-inch square pan. Combine sugar, sour cream, corn syrup, butter, and cocoa in a saucepan. Bring to a boil, stir-

ring constantly. Then cook, stirring occasionally, until tempera-
ture reaches 238°F. on the candy thermometer (soft ball stage).
Remove from heat. Stir in vanilla. Let cool to 110°F. (lukewarm).
Beat until fudge begins to thicken and loses its gloss. Stir in nuts.
Turn into the pan. Cool. Cut into squares. Makes about 36 pieces.

COCONUT POTATO FUDGE

¼ cup hot cooked mashed potatoes
1 teaspoon butter
2¼ cups sifted confectioners' sugar
1⅓ cups flaked coconut
½ teaspoon vanilla
dash of salt
2 squares unsweetened chocolate, 1-ounce size, melted

Butter an 8 by 4-inch loaf pan. Mix mashed potatoes and
butter in a bowl. Gradually add sugar, beating thoroughly after
each addition. Stir in coconut, vanilla, and salt. Pack in the loaf
pan; spread melted chocolate over the top. Chill until chocolate is
firm; then cut into squares. Makes 24 squares.

MAPLE FUDGE

2 cups maple syrup
1 tablespoon light corn syrup
¾ cup light cream
1 teaspoon vanilla
½ cup chopped butternuts
dash of salt

Butter an 8-inch square pan. Combine maple syrup, corn
syrup, light cream, and vanilla in a large heavy saucepan. Butter
the rim to prevent mixture from boiling over. Cook over medium
heat, stirring constantly, until mixture boils. Then continue
cooking over high heat without stirring, until liquid reaches 27°
higher temperature on the candy thermometer than the boiling
point of water in your locale. (To determine this, test thermometer in boiling water and then add 27°F. to the total.) Cool without
stirring to 110°F. Then stir circularly until the gloss barely begins
to disappear. Rapidly stir in nuts and salt and pour immediately
into the pan. Cool and cut into squares. Makes about 36 pieces.

MAPLE DIVINITY FUDGE

3 cups maple syrup
⅔ cup light corn syrup
2 egg whites
1 teaspoon baking powder
1 cup chopped walnuts

Butter an 8-inch square pan. Stir together maple syrup and corn syrup; boil until it forms a hard ball in cold water or reads 250°F. on the candy thermometer. Beat egg whites stiff. Pour candy mixture over stiffly beaten egg whites, beating constantly. When mixture stiffens in texture, stir in baking powder and chopped nuts; stir until thick enough to set. Pour mixture into the pan. Cool and then cut into squares. Makes about 36 pieces.

BROWN SUGAR FUDGE

¼ cup butter
½ cup brown sugar, firmly packed
1 pound confectioners' sugar
⅓ cup instant, nonfat dry milk
½ cup dark corn syrup
1 teaspoon vanilla
½ cup chopped nuts

Butter an 8-inch square pan. Melt butter and brown sugar in top of a 2-quart double boiler over boiling water. Meanwhile, sift confectioners' sugar and nonfat dry milk together; set aside. Stir corn syrup and vanilla into brown sugar mixture over boiling water. Stir in sifted dry ingredients, ½ at a time, stirring each time until mixture is well blended and smooth. Remove from boiling water. Mix in nuts. Turn into the pan. Cool. Cut into squares. Makes 36 pieces.

PATIENCE

3 cups sugar
2 cups warm milk
¼ cup butter
⅛ teaspoon salt
1 cup walnuts

Line an 8-inch square pan with waxed paper. In a heavy saucepan, cook 1 cup of the sugar over low to medium heat, stirring constantly until it is a golden brown. Gradually stir in 1 cup warm milk, and continue stirring until the caramelized sugar is dissolved. Then stir in the remaining 2 cups sugar, the remaining milk, butter, and salt; cook the mixture over low heat until the candy thermometer reaches 236°F. (soft ball stage). Remove from heat and beat mixture until it is smooth and begins to harden. Stir in nuts and press candy into the pan. Let stand at least 8 hours in a cold place before cutting into squares. Keep well wrapped to prevent drying out. Makes about 36 pieces.

COCONUT POTATO KISSES

¾ cup warm mashed potatoes
1 tablespoon butter
pinch of salt
1 teaspoon vanilla
1 pound confectioners' sugar
¾ pound shredded coconut

Cream together potato, butter, salt, and vanilla. Stir in the confectioners' sugar. Stir in shredded coconut. Drop by teaspoonful on waxed paper. Cool until set. Makes about 36 kisses.

PENUCHE

3 cups light brown sugar, firmly packed
¾ cup milk
1 tablespoon butter
1 tablespoon light corn syrup
¼ teaspoon salt
1 teaspoon vanilla
1 cup chopped nuts

Butter an 8-inch square pan. Combine brown sugar, milk, butter, corn syrup, and salt in a saucepan. Cook over medium heat, stirring constantly, until mixture boils. Continue cooking, stirring occasionally, until temperature reaches 238°F. on the candy thermometer (soft ball stage). Remove from heat. Cool to lukewarm (110°F.). Add vanilla. Beat until mixture holds its shape when dropped from spoon and loses its gloss. Quickly stir in nuts. Immediately pour into the pan. Cut into squares when cool. Makes about 36 pieces.

WALNUT PENUCHE

2 cups light brown sugar, firmly packed
⅓ cup cream
⅓ cup strong coffee
2 tablespoons butter
¼ teaspoon salt
1 cup chopped walnuts

Butter an 8-inch square pan. Combine brown sugar, cream and coffee; bring to a boil, stirring constantly. Cook without stirring to 238°F. (soft ball stage). Remove from heat; cool to 110°F. or until outside of pan is cool. Add butter and salt. Beat until thick and creamy. Add walnuts. Turn into the pan. Mark top into squares. Cool. Makes about 36 pieces.

Fondants and Creams

Fondant has the potential of being the prettiest of all candies you can make, because it can be flavored and tinted to your heart's delight. Stuff it into fruits or surround it with nuts, coat it with chocolate, or roll it into logs. Whatever your whim of the moment, the finished candy is bound to have eye appeal.

Cooked fondant is a combination of granulated sugar and water that is completely dissolved and then heated to 239°F. It is immediately cooled and then worked into a soft paste, flavored and tinted as you wish. In this chapter you will find an excellent recipe for basic cooked fondant. Do not eliminate the cream of tartar as it is the agent that separates the cohesiveness of the sugar and allows it to break down to become the creamy substance it should be. Any food acid (lemon juice, for example) may be substituted, but without that bit of acid you will be cooking something other than fondant.

Eliminating sugar crystals is most important too. If you permit them to remain, a chain reaction will be set up resulting in

47

a gritty end product. The recipe explains how to wash away the crystals and wet the area above the mixture to prevent further crystallization during cooking. It also helps to keep the stirring spoon and the thermometer scrupulously clean as you cook.

There are times when it is more expedient to use an uncooked type of fondant. For that reason, several versions are also included here. Do not substitute granulated sugar for the confectioners' or powdered variety in these recipes. Careful kneading is of utmost importance to keep the fondant mixture soft and pliable.

Make your own mints and tint them into pretty green, yellow, and pink circles with peppermint flavoring. See how easy they are to prepare, and you may want to make a larger quantity to give as hostess gifts or serve to friends at holiday times. To keep fondant creamy, store it in tightly closed containers.

Vegetable coloring is easily available in the baking section of your food market. Flavoring oils, aside from the more common vanilla and almond, may be more difficult to obtain. Ask your local pharmacy to order oil of peppermint, cinnamon, spearmint, wintergreen, and others for you. Small quantities will do as a few drops go a long way. Sometimes you may also want to color the fondant. You could use peppermint oil and then tint the mixture green, or knead a bit of butter in and then tint the mixture pale yellow. Let the artist in you be the judge, for this is one area of candymaking when you can be at your creative best.

BASIC COOKED FONDANT

3 cups sugar
2 cups water
¼ teaspoon cream of tartar

Combine sugar, water, and cream of tartar in a deep heavy saucepan. Stir until sugar is completely dissolved. With a clean wet sponge or pastry brush, wash away any clinging crystals from the rim of the saucepan down to the mixture, wetting the area completely. Cover the saucepan with a tight-fitting lid and cook for about 3 minutes.

Remove cover; insert candy thermometer and continue cooking, without stirring, until the thermometer registers exactly

Fondant at 239° F.

239°F. Just before it reaches this temperature pour cold water on the marble slab, china platter, or any smooth surface on which you intend to work. At 239°F., remove the mixture immediately and pour on the prepared surface, starting first with an outer circle and then filling in the middle. Let stand for 3 to 4 minutes until it begins to set. The mixture will be clear at this stage.

With a wide spatula, scrape the mixture to one side, then smooth it back to the area from which it was scraped. Work from every side towards the opposite side, keeping the mixture in perpetual motion. It will begin to thicken and turn white, and then suddenly turn into a firm mass. Knead this like dough for a minute or two.

Now separate the fondant into as many chunks as you wish to flavor differently. Add a few drops of flavoring oil to each chunk and knead to work the oil through. You may even work pieces of butter through at this point to make a creamier tasting butter fondant. Add instant coffee for a coffee flavor, liquefying it first with a little water. Add oil of peppermint, a fruit-flavored oil, or even a bit of vanilla extract. The choice is up to you.

When chunks are flavored and worked smooth coat your hands with cornstarch. Make ½-inch balls of the fondant. Let these stand for about an hour if you intend to coat with chocolate (see page 23). Fondant balls may also be rolled in confectioners' sugar; stuffed into dates, prunes, and figs; or placed between walnut halves.

If you wish to prepare the fondant and keep it for several weeks, snipping chunks of it as you please, store the fondant in a tightly covered crock at room temperature for best results. Makes about 1½ pounds of candy.

CHOCOLATE COCONUT FONDANT

2 cups sugar
1¼ cups water
2 tablespoons light corn syrup
dash of salt
2 tablespoons butter
1 teaspoon vanilla
4 squares semi-sweet chocolate, 1-ounce size, melted
¾ cup flaked coconut

Combine sugar, water, corn syrup, and salt in a saucepan. Cook over low heat, stirring constantly, until sugar is dissolved and mixture boils. Cover and cook for 3 minutes. Remove cover and continue boiling, without stirring, until a small amount of syrup forms a soft ball in cold water, 238°F. on the candy thermometer. Wipe down sides of pan occasionally with a spatula wrapped in damp cheesecloth. Remove from heat; add butter. Pour out on a cold wet platter, marble slab, or greased surface. Cool to lukewarm, 100°F. Then work mixture with a paddle or spatula until white and creamy (See directions for BASIC COOKED FONDANT, page 51). Add vanilla and knead until smooth. Shape into a ball, make an indentation in the top and pour in about one-fourth of the chocolate. Knead until chocolate is blended; repeat until all chocolate is used. Store in a tightly covered jar to ripen for several days before using. (If fondant begins to dry out, cover with a damp cloth.) Add coconut to ripened fondant and knead. Shape into 1-inch rolls, wrap in waxed paper and chill until firm. Cut into ¼-inch slices. Makes 36 pieces.

BASIC UNCOOKED FONDANT I

⅓ cup butter
⅓ cup light corn syrup
1 teaspoon vanilla
½ teaspoon salt
1 pound confectioners' sugar, sifted

Blend butter with the corn syrup, vanilla, and salt in a large mixing bowl. Add confectioners' sugar all at once and mix in, first with a spoon, then kneading with hands. Turn out onto a board and continue kneading until mixture is well blended and smooth. Store in a cool place. Shape as desired, forming into balls or rolling thin to cut into flat circles. Makes 1⅛ pounds of candy.

BASIC UNCOOKED FONDANT II

⅔ cup sweetened condensed milk
1 teaspoon vanilla
3½ cups confectioners' sugar, sifted

Blend sweetened condensed milk and vanilla. Add confectioners' sugar gradually and continue mixing until smooth and creamy. Makes about 1¼ pounds of candy.

CIRCUS BALLS

1 recipe BASIC UNCOOKED FONDANT
multi-colored sprinkles

Prepare fondant as directed. Shape into ½-inch balls. Roll in multicolored sprinkles. Makes 1⅛ pounds of candy.

MAPLE FONDANT

2 egg whites
1 cup maple syrup
3 cups sifted confectioners' sugar

Beat egg whites until stiff peaks form. Fold maple syrup through the egg whites; then add confectioners' sugar gradually, beating continuously until mixture becomes thick. Form into balls. Use as centers for dipping into melted unsweetened chocolate, if desired. Makes about 1½ pounds.

BUTTER FONDANT

⅓ cup butter
½ cup light corn syrup
1 pound confectioners' sugar, sifted
1 teaspoon vanilla

Lightly butter an 8-inch square pan. Mix together butter, corn syrup, and 2 cups of the sugar in a 3-quart saucepan. Cook over low heat, stirring constantly, until mixture comes to a full boil. Stir in remaining sugar. Remove from heat; stir in vanilla. Continue stirring until mixture holds shape. Pour into the baking pan; cool just enough to handle. Knead with lightly greased hands until smooth. (If candy hardens too much before kneading, work with spoon, then knead.) Knead in any desired flavoring and coloring. Shape as desired into balls or patties. Makes about 1⅛ pounds.

CHOCOLATE FONDANT

Sift ¼ cup cocoa with the confectioners' sugar; then follow recipe for BUTTER FONDANT.

MINT PATTIES

Flavor BUTTER FONDANT with peppermint or wintergreen; tint red or green with food coloring. Shape into patties.

RIBBON FONDANT

½ cup soft butter
3 tablespoons light corn syrup
¼ teaspoon salt
1½ teaspoons vanilla
1 pound confectioners' sugar
⅓ cup finely chopped nuts
few drops green food coloring
2 tablespoons finely chopped maraschino cherries
few drops red food coloring
¼ cup confectioners' sugar

Line a 10 by 4-inch loaf pan with aluminum foil. Cream

Ribbon fondant and opera creams.

butter with corn syrup, salt, and vanilla. Gradually beat in confectioners' sugar. Knead with fingers until smooth. Divide into 3 equal portions. Reserve one portion for the white layer. Flatten the second portion on a platter or waxed paper; sprinkle with nuts and green food coloring. Fold and knead mixture until nuts and coloring are evenly distributed. Add additional green food coloring if necessary. Then flatten the third portion in the same way; sprinkle with chopped cherries, red food coloring, and remaining ¼ cup confectioners' sugar. Fold and knead mixture until smooth and well mixed. If too soft, knead in a little additional confectioners' sugar. To assemble, press green fondant mixture into an even layer in bottom of pan. Top with white layer, then a layer of red. Cover and chill until firm. Remove from pan, remove foil, and cut into ½-inch slices. Then cut slices in half. Store in refrigerator. Makes about 1½ pounds.

BONBONS

1 recipe COOKED FONDANT
food coloring
nut pieces
fine granulated sugar
or
chocolate sprinkles
or
multi-colored sprinkles

Divide fondant and tint each portion with a few drops of food coloring to get desired shades. Shape into balls with a piece of nut in the center of each. Roll in sugar or in chocolate or multicolor sprinkles for decoration. Makes 1⅛ pounds of candy.

EASTER EGGS

1 recipe COOKED FONDANT
food coloring
1 cup confectioners' sugar
hot water

Prepare fondant as directed in the recipe; divide into portions and tint with a few drops of food coloring to obtain several

Spun sugar and Easter eggs.

different shades of pastel colors. Roll and shape into eggs of whatever size you choose. Sift confectioners' sugar into a bowl; stir in a little bit of hot water at a time, until mixture becomes the consistency of a thin icing. Carefully dip each egg into icing to coat thinly (icing may be divided and tinted into similar pastel colors if desired). Set on racks to dry. Makes about 1½ pounds of candy.

CHOCOLATE COVERED MINTS

1 recipe COOKED FONDANT
1 teaspoon spearmint extract
3 drops green food coloring
4 tablespoons butter
8 squares semi-sweet chocolate, 1-ounce size

Prepare fondant as directed in the recipe, adding spearmint extract and green food coloring when you add the vanilla. Shape into 1-inch balls, then flatten. Set aside. Melt butter and semi-sweet chocolate squares in the top of a double boiler over hot, but not boiling, water. Cool slightly. Using two spoons, dip patties into chocolate and coat completely. Place on waxed paper. Set in a cool place until firm. Store covered in refrigerator. Makes 45 mint patties.

PARTY MINTS

3 egg whites
1 tablespoon light corn syrup
9 cups (about) sifted confectioners' sugar
1 teaspoon peppermint extract
food coloring, if desired

Beat egg whites until foamy. Add corn syrup and beat until stiff enough to form peaks when beaters are raised, but not dry. Gradually add confectioners' sugar, beating well with a wooden spoon after each addition. Add flavoring and food coloring, if desired, after the first addition of sugar. Continue to add sugar until the mixture holds shape, is very stiff, and is not sticky to the touch. Continue blending by kneading with hands until smooth. Divide mixture into thirds. Between two pieces of waxed paper, roll out each third into a ¼ to ⅛-inch thickness. Refrigerate one hour. Remove the top layer of waxed paper; cut into desired shapes using a small biscuit cutter or miniature cookie cutters. (Decorate with leaves and flowers by using a colored confectioners' sugar frosting.) Harden at room temperature for several hours, then store in a covered container. Makes about 11 dozen 1¼-inch circles.

NOTE: Combine 1 cup sifted confectioners' sugar with a tablespoon or so of hot water, adding water only until sugar is soft and manageable. Stir in desired food coloring and use with a cake decorator to make leaves and flowers.

MORAVIAN MINTS

3 cups confectioners' sugar
1 cup water
12 drops oil of peppermint or wintergreen
green food coloring (optional)

Combine sugar and water; boil together until a small amount dropped in water forms a soft ball, or 238°F. on the candy thermometer. Add flavoring. Add coloring if desired. Remove from heat and beat until mixture thickens. Drop from spoon or oiled funnel to form thin patties on waxed paper. This is easier to do if you set mixture over hot water as you spoon it. Makes about 48 mints.

MINT CREAMS

⅓ cup butter
⅓ cup light corn syrup
1 teaspoon peppermint or wintergreen flavoring
½ teaspoon salt
1 pound confectioners' sugar, sifted
red or green food coloring

Blend butter with the corn syrup, flavoring, and salt in a large mixing bowl. Add confectioners' sugar all at once and mix, first with a spoon, then by kneading with hands. Tint with either red or green food coloring. Shape into balls or roll thin and cut into flat circles. Makes 1⅛ pounds candy.

LEMON CREAMS

⅓ *cup butter*
⅓ *cup light corn syrup*
1 *teaspoon lemon extract*
½ *teaspoon salt*
1 *pound confectioners' sugar*
yellow food coloring

Blend butter with the corn syrup, lemon extract, and salt in a large mixing bowl. Add confectioners' sugar all at once and mix in, first with a spoon, then kneading with hands. Knead in food coloring until evenly distributed. Shape into balls or roll thin and cut into flat circles. Makes 1⅛ pounds candy.

ORANGE CREAMS

⅓ *cup butter*
⅓ *cup light corn syrup*
2 *teaspoons orange extract*
½ *teaspoon salt*
1 *pound confectioners' sugar, sifted*
orange food coloring

Blend butter with the corn syrup, orange extract, and salt in a large mixing bowl. Add confectioners' sugar all at once and mix in, first with a spoon, then by kneading with hands. Knead in food color until evenly distributed. Shape into balls or roll thin and cut into flat circles. Makes 1⅛ pounds candy.

CHOCOLATE CREAMS

⅓ *cup butter*
⅓ *cup light corn syrup*
1 *teaspoon vanilla*
½ *teaspoon salt*
1 *pound confectioners' sugar*
¼ *cup cocoa*

Blend butter with the corn syrup, vanilla, and salt in a large mixing bowl. Sift confectioners' sugar and cocoa together; add all at once to the mixture in bowl, mixing first with a spoon, then kneading with hands. Turn out onto a board and continue kneading until mixture is well blended and smooth. Store in a cool place. Roll into balls or roll thin and cut into flat circles. Makes about 1⅓ pounds of candy.

FRUIT CREAMS

½ cup light corn syrup
⅓ cup butter
1 package fruit-flavored gelatin, 3-ounce size
1 pound confectioners' sugar, sifted
colored sugar (optional)
multi-colored sprinkles (optional)
chocolate sprinkles (optional)

Butter a 9-inch square pan. Combine corn syrup, butter, and gelatin in a saucepan. Cook over low heat, stirring constantly, until butter has melted and gelatin is completely dissolved. Stir in confectioners' sugar, one-third at a time. Remove from heat. Turn into the pan. Let cool enough to handle, then form into a ball. Pull off small amounts and shape as desired. Roll in colored sugar, multi-colored decorators, or chocolate sprinkles. Makes 1½ pounds of candy.

NOTE: This mixture may also be used as stuffing for dates and prunes.

GRAND OPERA CREAMS

2 cups sugar
¼ teaspoon salt
1 cup light cream
2 tablespoons butter
2 tablespoons light corn syrup
1½ teaspoons vanilla
2 squares, 2-ounce size semi-sweet chocolate
2 teaspoons solid vegetable shortening

Combine sugar, salt, cream, butter, and corn syrup in a heavy 2½-quart saucepan. Bring to a boil, stirring constantly. Cook at a gentle boil, stirring frequently, until the mixture reaches 238°F. on the candy thermometer (soft ball stage).

Making cream candies, 1890.

Remove from heat and cool, without stirring, until mixture is 110°F. Add vanilla and beat vigorously until candy is thick and loses its gloss. Quickly drop by teaspoon into mounds on waxed paper. If the candy gets too stiff and dry before this is completed, knead each dropped candy between fingers or roll between the palms of the hands. It will soften and become more attractive. Let candy stand until firm to the touch. Meanwhile, melt chocolate in the top of a double boiler over simmering water. Stir in vegetable shortening. Spoon a small amount of chocolate glaze over each cream. Let stand until set. Wrap in plastic and store in refrigerator. Makes about 24 candies.

COCONUT CREAM CANDY

1½ cups sugar
½ cup water
2 teaspoons corn syrup
1½ cups grated coconut
¼ cup well drained crushed canned pineapple, if desired
food coloring, if desired

Combine sugar, water, and syrup in a heavy saucepan. Cook the mixture over medium heat until it reaches 248°F. on the candy thermometer (firm ball stage). Wash down the sides of the saucepan with a pastry brush dipped in hot water. Remove from heat, stir in coconut and pineapple. Gently boil the mixture until it is very thick, between 226°F. and 236°F. Remove from heat and beat the mixture until it becomes creamy. Blend in food coloring. When the candy is thick enough, drop from a teaspoon onto waxed paper. Makes about 1 pound.

CHOCOLATE CANDY ROLL

½ pound semi-sweet chocolate
2 tablespoons water
¼ cup light corn syrup
⅛ teaspoon salt
1 recipe BASIC UNCOOKED FONDANT

Heat chocolate and water in a double boiler top over boiling water, until chocolate is melted. Remove from heat. Add corn syrup and salt; beat until well blended. Pour onto two 15 by 6-inch sheets of waxed paper. Chill well.

Meanwhile, prepare BASIC UNCOOKED FONDANT as directed. Roll fondant out to cover two 15 by 6-inch pieces of waxed paper. Remove chocolate layers from refrigerator. Flip fondant layer on top of each chocolate layer, removing waxed paper. Roll up each roll tightly, starting at one long side of each. Chill well before slicing. Store in refrigerator. Makes about 2 pounds of candy.

MOCHA LOGS

⅓ cup butter
⅓ cup light corn syrup
1 teaspoon vanilla
½ teaspoon salt
1 pound confectioners' sugar, sifted
2 teaspoons instant coffee powder
chocolate sprinkles

Blend butter with corn syrup, vanilla, and salt in a large mixing bowl. Add confectioners' sugar all at once and mix in, first with a spoon, then kneading with hands. Add coffee powder and

knead well. Shape into rolls, about 2 inches long and ½ inch thick.
Roll in chocolate sprinkles. Makes about 1⅓ pounds of candy.

CANDY CORN

> 1 cup sugar
> ⅔ cup light corn syrup
> ⅓ cup butter
> 1 teaspoon vanilla
> 2½ cups sifted confectioners' sugar
> ⅓ cup instant, nonfat dry milk
> ¼ teaspoon salt
> yellow food coloring

Popcorn candies and hard candies.

Combine sugar, corn syrup, and butter in a medium-sized saucepan. Bring to a boil over medium heat, stirring constantly, until sugar is dissolved. Turn heat to very low and boil gently for 5 minutes, stirring occasionally. Remove from heat. Add vanilla. Meanwhile, combine confectioners' sugar, dry milk, and salt; add all at once to cooked mixture, stirring until mixture is plastic and cool enough to handle. Continue mixing and kneading until candy is stiff enough to hold its shape when molded. More confectioners' sugar may be kneaded in, if necessary. Color about two-thirds of the mixture a deep yellow, by adding several drops of food coloring at a time. Make large-sized kernels of corn by shaping a triangular piece of white candy, about 1 inch on all sides. Then shape a rectangular piece of yellow, about 1 by 1¼ inches. Join the two pieces and mold to resemble the corn. Let stand until set; wrap individual pieces in waxed paper and store in a tight container. Make smaller kernels the same way, reducing the size as desired. Makes about 1¾ pounds of candy.

MAPLE SUGAR CANDY

2 pounds maple sugar
¼ teaspoon cream of tartar
1 cup water

Combine maple sugar, cream of tartar, and water in a large heavy saucepan; butter the rim to prevent the mixture from boiling over. Bring to a boil, stirring constantly, and continue cooking until the candy thermometer reaches 234°F. (soft ball stage). Cool. Then work with a wooden paddle until mixture becomes thick and creamy. Pour into twelve 2-inch muffin tins, or into maple sugar molds. When cold, invert and remove candies. Makes about 2 pounds of candy.

Caramels, Divinity, and Nougats

Remember these chewy delights? They may not be the best looking of all candies, but for real old-fashioned creamy goodness and melt-in-the-mouth succulence, they would win a prize at any state fair.

Caramels are made from cooked sugar, corn syrup, and some form of cream or butter. They are rather sticky when you get to the cutting stage, so be sure to use a very sharp knife and press firmly as you slice the squares. If they are to be stored, wrap them well in waxed paper to keep them moist and tender. And if you plan to use them as centers for chocolate dipping, cut them into smaller squares and dip as soon as possible. These do not have to be wrapped, as the chocolate coating will form a tight seal around the caramel—keeping it soft and tasty for many months.

Divinity is made by pouring a cooked syrup into well-beaten egg whites. This produces a fluffy sticky mixture that is best handled by dropping spoonfuls on heavily waxed paper, as soon as the mixture has been smoothly combined. You really have to work fast, as the mixture hardens very rapidly and cannot be shaped once it has set. Do not wrap these candies, but store them in a tightly closed container as soon as the pieces have set firmly.

Nougat has a bonus inside: not only is it chewy, but it also contains fruit and nuts. The same glacéed fruits used for fruit cake may be used in nougat too, providing a harlequin of color with every bite.

If you analyze the recipes for nougats with those for divinity, you will see that the first part of the preparations are similar. But nougat is a more complicated procedure, and requires a second stage of cooking and beating. It is well worth the time spent, but important to remember that it does take extra time and care to produce a fine quality of nougat. These may also be chocolate coated as they hold as firm a shape as the caramels. If they are not dipped in chocolate, they must be wrapped in waxed paper at once. Then pop the wrapped candies in a covered container for longer lasting freshness.

Do not be surprised if you have visions of quilting bees and wood burning stoves as you sink your teeth into the fruits of your candymaking session of caramels, divinity, or heavenly nougats.

CREAMY CARAMELS

2 cups light cream
2 cups sugar
1 cup light or dark corn syrup
½ teaspoon salt
⅛ cup butter
½ cup chopped nuts
1 teaspoon vanilla

Lightly butter an 8-inch square pan. Heat cream to luke-warm in a large heavy saucepan. Pour out 1 cup; set aside. Add sugar, corn syrup, and salt to the remaining cream in the saucepan. Cook over medium heat, stirring constantly, until mixture boils. Add remaining 1 cup cream very slowly, so mixture does not stop boiling. Cook for 5 minutes, stirring constantly. Stir in butter, about 1 teaspoon at a time. Turn heat low; boil gently, stirring constantly, until temperature reaches 248°F. or until a small amount of mixture dropped into very cold water forms a firm ball

Left, cutting caramels, 1890. Right, creamy caramels.

which does not flatten on removal from water. Remove from heat. Gently mix in nuts and vanilla; let stand 10 minutes. Stir just enough to distribute nuts. Pour into one corner of the pan, letting mixture flow to its own level in pan. (Do not scrape cooking pan.) Cool to room temperature. Turn out onto cutting board. Cool. Mark off into ¾-inch squares. Cut with a large sharp knife. Wrap each caramel in waxed paper to store. Makes about 2 pounds of candy.

CREAMY CHOCOLATE CARAMELS

1 recipe CREAMY CARAMELS
4 ounces unsweetened chocolate

Proceed with recipe directions, adding chocolate with the nuts and vanilla.

CREAMY RAISIN CARAMELS

1 recipe CREAMY CARAMELS
1 cup chopped raisins

Proceed with recipe directions, adding chopped raisins with nuts and vanilla.

VANILLA CARAMELS

2 cups sugar
2 cups half-and-half cream
1¾ cups light corn syrup
½ cup butter
⅛ teaspoon salt
1 tablespoon vanilla
1 cup chopped nuts (optional)

Butter a 9-inch square pan. Mix sugar, half-and-half cream, corn syrup, butter, and salt in a heavy 4-quart saucepan. Cook over medium heat, stirring constantly, until mixture comes to a boil and sugar is dissolved. Continue cooking, stirring frequently, until temperature on the candy thermometer reaches 244°F. (firm ball stage). Remove from heat and stir in vanilla and nuts. Immediately pour into the pan. Let stand until firm. Chill about one hour, then cut into squares. Wrap each square in waxed paper or plastic wrap. Makes about 2½ pounds of candy.

COBBLESTONE CARAMELS

1 cup semi-sweet chocolate mini-chips
3 cups sugar
1 cup light cream
1 cup milk
⅔ cup light corn syrup
1 cup butter
1 tablespoon vanilla

Line bottom and sides of a 9-inch square pan with aluminum foil; lightly butter sides only. Sprinkle chocolate mini-chips evenly in pan. Combine sugar, cream, milk, corn syrup, and butter in a heavy 4-quart saucepan. Place over medium heat, stirring constantly until mixture boils. Cook to 240°F. on the candy thermometer, stirring occasionally. Reduce heat to low and stir constantly to avoid scorching; continue to cook to 246°F. (firm ball stage). Remove from heat at once and let stand for 2 minutes.

Stir in vanilla; slowly pour over chocolate chips in pan. Let stand several hours or overnight. Invert pan and remove aluminum foil from candy. Cut into 1-inch squares. Wrap individually in waxed paper. Makes about 60 candies.

MOLASSES CARAMELS

2 cups brown sugar
1 cup molasses
1 cup semi-sweet chocolate bits
⅓ cup butter

Butter a 7½ by 12-inch pan. Combine sugar, molasses, chocolate bits, and butter in a large saucepan; bring to a boil and cook for about 15 minutes, or until the mixture when dropped off a spoon begins to "hair." Pour into the pan. Cool and cut into squares. Makes about 80 pieces.

TURTLETTES

1½ cups coarsely chopped pecans
1 cup light cream
1 cup sugar
½ cup light corn syrup
¼ teaspoon salt
3 tablespoons butter
½ teaspoon vanilla
1 package semi-sweet chocolate chips, 6-ounce size

Spread pecans on a greased baking sheet. Butter another baking sheet. Heat cream to lukewarm in a heavy 2-quart saucepan. Pour out ½ cup of the warm cream; reserve. Add sugar, light corn syrup, and salt to the remaining cream in the saucepan. Cook over medium heat, stirring constantly, until mixture boils. Stir in reserved cream very slowly, so mixture does not stop boiling. Cook 5 minutes, stirring constantly. Stir in butter, about 1 teaspoon at a time. Reduce heat to low. Boil gently, stirring constantly, until temperature reaches 248°F. on the candy thermometer (firm ball stage). Remove from heat. Gently stir in vanilla. Cool caramel mixture slightly. Drop teaspoonfuls of caramel onto chopped pecans. As the caramel sets, remove and place on another baking sheet to cool. If the caramel stiffens, it may be reheated over low heat, stirring constantly. Melt semi-sweet chocolate chips over hot, but not boiling, water. Stir until smooth. Spread chocolate over each turtlette. Let chocolate set in a cool place away from drafts. Do not refrigerate or chocolate will turn gray. Wrap in plastic film when set. Makes about 44 two-inch candies.

CHOCOLATE CARAMELS

2 cups sugar
¾ cup light corn syrup
⅔ cup butter
3 squares baking chocolate, 1-ounce size, grated
⅔ cup milk
1 teaspoon powdered cinnamon

Butter an 8-inch square pan. Combine all ingredients except cinnamon in a deep heavy saucepan. Bring to a boil, stirring constantly. Continue stirring and boil until candy thermometer reaches 258°F. (firm ball stage). Add cinnamon. Stir a moment longer, then remove from heat and pour into the pan. Mark into squares when cool, and cut into squares when cold. Wrap in waxed paper. Makes about 64 candies.

QUICK CHOCOLATE CARAMELS

3 cups sugar
½ cup butter
1 cup milk
1 square baking chocolate, 1-ounce size, melted
1 tablespoon vanilla

Butter an 8-inch square pan. Combine sugar, butter, milk, and melted chocolate together in a heavy saucepan. Cook and stir constantly until temperature reaches 246°F. on the candy thermometer (firm ball stage). Remove from heat. Beat mixture until cool. Add vanilla. Pour into the pan. Cut into 1-inch squares. Makes 64 pieces.

MARSHMALLOW CARAMELS

1½ cups sugar
¾ cup light corn syrup
½ cup milk
1 tablespoon butter
½ teaspoon vanilla
1 cup marshmallows

Butter an 8-inch square pan. Combine sugar, syrup, and milk in a saucepan. Boil, stirring, until 264°F. (hard ball stage). Add butter, remove from heat and let stand for 3 minutes. Add vanilla and chopped marshmallows; beat until creamy. Marshmallows should appear as small white flakes throughout the mixture. Pour into the pan. Cut into squares when cold. Wrap in waxed paper. Makes about 64 pieces.

DIVINITY

2½ cups sugar
½ cup light corn syrup
½ cup water
¼ teaspoon salt
2 egg whites
1 teaspoon vanilla
1 cup coarsely chopped walnuts or pecans (optional)

Mix together sugar, corn syrup, water, and salt in a 2-quart saucepan. Cook over medium heat, stirring constantly, until mixture comes to a boil. Reduce heat; cook without stirring, until temperature reaches 248°F. on the candy thermometer (firm ball stage). While you are waiting for the thermometer to reach 248°F., beat egg whites in large bowl until stiff but not dry. While beating constantly on the high speed of an electric mixer, slowly pour about one-half the hot syrup over beaten egg whites. Then cook the remaining syrup to 272°F. (soft crack stage). Beating constantly, pour this hot syrup over first mixture, about 1 tablespoon at a time, beating well after each addition. Continue beating until the mixture begins to lose its gloss and a small amount of it holds a soft peak when dropped from a spoon. (If mixture becomes too stiff for mixer, beat with a wooden spoon.)

Mix in vanilla and nuts. Drop by teaspoonfuls onto waxed paper. Makes about 1¼ pounds or about 48 pieces.

NOTE: Divinity may also be poured into an 8-inch square, buttered pan.

CHOCOLATE DIVINITY

Follow recipe for DIVINITY. When the mixture begins to lose its gloss after the last addition of hot syrup, reduce the mixer speed to low. Add 2 (1-ounce) squares unsweetened chocolate, melted; then add vanilla and nuts, if desired. Beat until mixture holds its shape when dropped from a spoon.

CHOCOLATE MINT DIVINITY

Follow recipe for CHOCOLATE DIVINITY, substituting ½ teaspoon peppermint extract for vanilla.

COFFEE DIVINITY

Follow recipe for DIVINITY, but add 2 teaspoons instant coffee powder after the last addition of hot syrup and beat until mixture begins to lose its gloss.

MARBLE DIVINITY

Follow recipe for DIVINITY, omitting nuts and gently folding in ½ cup semi-sweet chocolate chips instead.

CHERRY DIVINITY

3 cups sugar
¾ cup light corn syrup
¾ cup hot water
⅓ cup egg whites (about 2 eggs) at room temperature
1 teaspoon vanilla
¼ teaspoon salt
½ cup chopped candied cherries
½ cup chopped walnuts or pecans

In a 2-quart saucepan, combine sugar, corn syrup, and water. Cook to 260°F. on the candy thermometer (hard ball stage), stir-

Clockwise from top: frosted nuts, taffy, rock candy, patience, divinity, and pralines.

ring occasionally. Remove from heat. At once beat egg whites until they cling to bowl; then continue beating 30 seconds more. Pour hot syrup very slowly over the egg whites, beating constantly at high speed. (If the syrup is added too quickly the whites will cook and form lumps.) Continue beating at high speed until candy begins to stand up. It may take from 5 to 15 minutes. Quickly add vanilla, salt, candied cherries, and nuts. Drop from a buttered spoon on waxed paper. (Divinity may also be poured into an 8-inch square buttered pan.) Flatten the top and store covered in the refrigerator until firm. Cut into squares. Makes about 60 pieces.

HONEY NOUGAT

½ cup honey
3 cups sugar
⅔ cup boiling water
2 egg whites
⅔ cup chopped nuts
⅔ cup chopped candied cherries

Line a 9-inch square pan with waxed paper or aluminum foil. Combine the honey, sugar, and boiling water in a heavy saucepan; bring to a boil, stirring constantly, until candy thermometer reaches 230° F. (soft ball stage). Beat egg whites until stiff; pour ⅔ cup of the syrup into the egg whites, beating while pouring. Cook the remainder of the syrup to 265° F. (hard ball stage). Pour into the egg white mixture, beating continuously. Beat until the candy begins to thicken. Add nuts and candied cherries. Pour into the pan. Cut into oblong pieces, about 1¼ by 1-inch. Makes about 48 pieces.

CHOCOLATE CHIP NOUGAT

Part 1:
1 cup sugar
⅔ cup light corn syrup
2 tablespoons water
¼ cup egg whites, at room temperature
Part 2:
2 cups sugar
1¼ cups light corn syrup
¼ cup butter, melted
2 teaspoons vanilla
2 cups chopped nuts
1 cup semi-sweet chocolate mini-chips
2 to 3 drops red food coloring

Line the bottom and sides of a 9-inch square pan with aluminum foil and butter well. Combine 1 cup sugar with ⅔ cup corn syrup and 2 tablespoons water in a small heavy saucepan. Place over medium heat, stirring constantly, until sugar dissolves; then cook without stirring. When candy thermometer reaches 230° F., start beating egg whites until stiff, but not dry. When syrup reaches 238°F. (soft ball stage), add syrup in a thin stream to the beaten egg whites, beating constantly with the mixer at high speed. Continue beating for about 4 to 5 minutes or until mixture becomes very thick. Cover and set aside.

Using ingredients for Part 2, combine sugar and corn syrup in a heavy 2-quart saucepan. Place over medium heat, stirring constantly until sugar dissolves. Cook without stirring to 275°F. on the candy thermometer (soft crack stage). Pour hot syrup all at once over the reserved ingredients of Part 1; blend with a wooden spoon. Stir in butter and vanilla; add nuts and blend thoroughly. Turn one-half of the mixture into the prepared pan; press evenly in pan. Sprinkle chocolate mini-chips evenly over candy in pan. Add red food coloring to remaining one-half candy in the bowl; blend quickly and turn into pan. With buttered fingers, carefully spread this top layer of candy over the chocolate mini-chips. Let candy stand several hours or overnight. Invert the pan and remove the aluminum foil from the nougat. Cut nougat into 1 by ¾-inch pieces. Wrap individually in waxed paper. Makes about 84 candies.

PULLING CANDY.

Pulling candy, 1890.

Taffies

Few things promote laughter and group activity as well as an old-fashioned taffy pull. Suggest it the next time you want an inexpensive evening that will also recapture the simple fun of long ago.

The secret to making good taffy is to cool it quickly and then pull it properly. Ideally the pulling should be done by two people—one to hold his or her hands in the position of a hook, and the other to throw the elastic strip of taffy back and forth over them. The more delicately the candy is handled, the lighter it will become.

Never twist taffy as too much air is lost that way. Instead fold it back straight after each pull. The object is to get a whitish, porous condition by carefully stretching the candy and keeping it folded back upon itself. If another person is not available, a large hardware hook, fastened to a wall or cabinet, will serve the same purpose although it will not be half as much fun. Just hang the taffy at its central point over the hook, like a damp towel, and pull straight towards yourself on both sides. Remove from the hook, fold ends together, place center over the hook again, and repeat the action by pulling the taffy straight with two hands. Do this over and over until the taffy turns very light-colored and porous.

Another method for do-it-yourselfers, is to grasp the taffy in the left hand, palm upwards, and pull it towards yourself with your right hand. Keep working it in this way, being careful to keep the taffy straight.

Very small amounts of taffy may be pulled with the thumb and index fingers of both hands. Whatever method you choose to use, remember to butter your hands first (margarine will do, too), so the taffy won't stick to your fingers. When the mass is fluffy and full of air, it will no longer have a plastic feel to it. Fold it into a long oval shape and lay the taffy on a smooth warm surface. Start rolling the right side of the oval with the heels of the palms of your hands—roll into a thin rope. For smaller amounts, shape the taffy with your fingers if you prefer.

Cut or pinch off bite-sized pieces of taffy. Work quickly before the taffy hardens. Wrap in waxed paper to keep the candy fresh: Store in tightly closed containers until ready to serve.

TAFFY

1 cup light corn syrup
½ cup sugar
1 tablespoon vinegar
1 teaspoon butter
flavoring

Lightly butter a dish or platter. Combine syrup, sugar, vinegar, and butter in a saucepan. Boil until firm, 252°F. on the candy thermometer. Pour onto the dish. When cool enough to handle, add several drops of whatever flavoring you desire. Pull with thumbs and forefingers until taffy is light. Pull off pieces and wrap in small squares of waxed paper. Makes about ½ pound.

CHOCOLATE TAFFY

2 cups dark corn syrup
¼ cup water
2½ ounces unsweetened chocolate

¼ *teaspoon salt*
1 *tablespoon butter*
¼ *teaspoon vanilla*

Butter an 8-inch square pan. Combine corn syrup, water, chocolate, and salt in a saucepan. Bring to a boil over medium heat, stirring constantly. Continue cooking, stirring almost constantly, until temperature reaches 260° F. on the candy thermometer (hard ball stage). Remove from heat. Add butter and vanilla. Stir only enough to mix. Pour into the pan. Let cool enough to handle. Pull candy with fingers until satin-like in finish, light in color and elastic. Pull into long strips about ½-inch in diameter. Cut into 1-inch pieces. Wrap in waxed paper. Makes about 1 pound.

NOTE: To prepare pan taffy, pour taffy mixture into a greased 8-inch square pan. Cool. Cut into squares.

MINT TAFFY

4 *cups sugar*
1 *cup water*
½ *cup light corn syrup*
¼ *cup dark corn syrup*
1 *tablespoon butter*
1 *teaspoon white vinegar*
¾ *teaspoon cream of tartar*
2 *teaspoons mint extract*
2 to 3 *drops green food coloring (optional)*

Butter a 9-inch square pan. Mix together sugar, water, corn syrups, butter, vinegar, and cream of tartar. Bring to a boil over medium heat, stirring constantly, until sugar dissolves. Continue cooking without stirring, until temperature reaches 270° F. on the candy thermometer (soft crack stage). Remove from heat. Stir in mint extract and food coloring, if desired. Pour into the pan. Let stand until cool enough to handle. Pull until taffy has a satin-like finish and light color. Pull into strips ½-inch wide. Cut into 1-inch pieces with scissors. Wrap pieces individually in waxed paper. Makes about 2 pounds of taffy.

TAFFY STRIPES

2 cups sugar
1½ cups light corn syrup
1 cup water
½ teaspoon peppermint flavoring
¼ teaspoon red or green food coloring

Butter two 8-inch square pans. Combine sugar, corn syrup, and water in a saucepan. Bring to a boil over medium heat, stirring constantly, until sugar dissolves. Continue cooking without stirring until candy thermometer reaches 260°F. (hard ball stage). Remove from heat. Quickly stir in flavoring. Pour one-half the mixture into the pan. Quickly add coloring to remaining mixture and pour into another pan. When cool enough to handle, pull each taffy separately until it has a satin-like finish and light color. Pull into long ropes; twist and pull the red, or green, and white taffies together (barber pole fashion) until strands do not separate. Pull into long strips, ½-inch in diameter, cut into 1-inch pieces with scissors. Wrap individually in waxed paper. Makes about 1 pound of candy.

NOTE: To make candy canes, use only red food coloring. After pulling the striped taffy into long ½-inch strips, as directed above, cut into 6 or 8-inch lengths and shape into candy canes.

BLACK WALNUT TAFFY

1½ cups sugar
½ cup light molasses
½ cup water
1½ tablespoons vinegar
¼ teaspoon cream of tartar
4 tablespoons melted butter
⅛ teaspoon baking soda
½ cup finely chopped black walnuts

Oil a marble slab or heavy stainless steel pan. In a heavy saucepan, combine sugar, molasses, water, and vinegar. Cook over medium heat, stirring continuously, until mixture comes to the boiling point and the sugar is melted. Add cream of tartar. Continue boiling, stirring constantly, until temperature reaches 256°F. on the candy thermometer (hard ball stage). Stir in butter, baking soda, and nuts. Pour onto the marble slab or into a heavy stainless steel pan. As the candy cools around the sides, fold toward the center. When it is cool enough to handle, pull until porous and light colored, using your fingertips and thumbs. Shape into a rope. Cut into 1-inch pieces with a pair of scissors or heavy knife. Let harden and wrap tightly in individual pieces of waxed paper. Makes about 1 pound.

NOTE: If taffy becomes too hard to pull, warm in the oven for a few minutes.

SALT WATER TAFFY

> 2 cups sugar
> 1 tablespoon cornstarch
> 1 cup light corn syrup
> 2 tablespoons butter
> ¾ cup water
> 1 teaspoon salt
> flavoring
> food coloring

Butter a platter or cookie sheet. Put the sugar and cornstarch into a saucepan. Add corn syrup, butter, and water. Stir until the boiling point is reached. Then boil without stirring, until the candy thermometer reaches 266°F. (firm ball stage). Add salt and pour on the prepared platter. When cool enough to handle, pull until the batch is light colored. Divide the mixture into separate portions. Flavor and color each portion as desired by pulling the additions through each portion. Portions may be flavored with lemon, orange, peppermint, lime, strawberry, or pineapple, and colored to correspond. Pull off bite-sized pieces and wrap in waxed paper. Store in a tightly closed container. Makes about 1 pound.

BUTTERSCOTCH TAFFY

> 1 cup sugar
> 2 tablespoons molasses
> 1 tablespoon vinegar
> 1 tablespoon water
> ¼ cup butter

Butter a marble slab or a cookie sheet. Combine sugar, molasses, vinegar, water, and butter in a large saucepan. Stir until mixture begins to boil; continue boiling and stirring until candy thermometer reaches 260°F. (hard ball stage). Pour onto prepared surface. Cool. Pull until light and porous. Twist off pieces and wrap in waxed paper. Makes about ½ pound.

TIDDLYWINKS

1 recipe BUTTERSCOTCH TAFFY
2 squares unsweetened chocolate, 1-ounce size

Butter a cookie sheet. Prepare taffy as directed. Melt chocolate in the top of a double boiler over hot, but not boiling, water. Break butterscotch taffy into small pieces. With a two-tined fork, dip each piece into the melted chocolate and coat completely. Put on the cookie sheet to dry.

PULLED MAPLE CANDY

2 cups maple syrup
butter

Butter a large pan or platter. Pour maple syrup into a heavy saucepan. Butter the top inch of the inside rim. Boil at medium heat without stirring, until candy thermometer reaches 300°F. (hard crack stage). Pour immediately into the pan or platter. Cool just until it can be handled. Then butter hands lightly. Pull syrup away from pan edges and pick it up in a ball. Pull like taffy, stretching, folding back on itself, and stretching again until it turns light (nearly white). It will take about 15 minutes of pulling. The candy will stick less if pulled in a cool room or even outdoors. Finally pull candy into ropes on waxed paper. Cut with scissors into bite-sized pieces and wrap in small pieces of waxed paper. Makes about ½ pound.

PULLED MINTS

1½ cups sugar
½ cup water
2 tablespoons light corn syrup
¼ teaspoon oil of peppermint
red or green food coloring, if desired

Butter a 9-inch square pan. Combine sugar, water, and syrup in a 2-quart saucepan. Cook over low heat, stirring constantly, until sugar is dissolved. Cover and cook for 3 minutes to allow steam to wash sugar crystals from sides of pan. Remove cover and cook without stirring until mixture reaches 260°F. (hard ball stage). (If necessary, during cooking, remove sugar crystals from sides of pan with a spatula wrapped with damp cheesecloth.) Remove mixture from heat. Pour into the pan and let stand until cool enough to handle. Pour oil of peppermint, and several drops of food coloring, if desired, into center of candy. Fold the corners over to center. Pull the candy with your fingers until it has a satin-like finish and is a light color. Pull into long strips, ½-inch in diameter, then cut into ½- to 1-inch pieces. Layer pieces in a container with waxed paper between each layer. Cover. Store overnight or until mints become creamy. Makes about ½ pound of candy.

UNPULLED TAFFY

1 cup molasses
1 cup sugar
1 tablespoon butter

Butter an 8-inch square pan. Combine molasses, sugar, and butter in a large saucepan. Bring to a boil and then cook for about 20 minutes, stirring constantly, until candy thermometer registers 264°F. (hard ball stage). Pour into the pan and mark into squares at once. Cool. Cut or break taffy at the marks. Makes 64 one-inch squares.

DELICIOUS
KARO
RECIPES

Hard Candies and Candied Apples

All-day suckers used to bring lots of contentment to the lucky lickers. And do you remember the sticky joy of the first bite into a candied apple? Those moments can be recaptured with a few simple ingredients that are probably on your kitchen shelf right now.

Hard candies are easy to make if you follow the directions carefully. You are going to cook the sugar mixture to the "hard crack" stage. At this stage, it is of the utmost importance to prevent crystallization as the high heat propels the temperature towards the top range of the candy thermometer. The results of cooking should be a clear, glass-like mass in which most of the liquid has been lost to evaporation. Score the small candies, form the lollipops, or dip the apples—with a spirit of speed—after you have colored and flavored the hard crack candy. The speed is necessary to prevent tiny air bubbles and premature hardening.

Although fondant candies are easily tinted and flavored with a small amount of color and extract, hard candies require a good

83

deal more coloring and flavoring in order to have a distinct character. Colors may be added by drops or in the form of food paste, which is available at confectionary supply establishments. Flavorings may be purchased at your food market if they are also used for popular baking recipes, or at your pharmacy if they are used to disguise nasty medicines too. Start by purchasing small quantities, so you can experiment with the combinations that might please you.

Here are some suggested combinations of flavors and colors to consider:

peppermint .... pink
cinnamon, cherry................. red
lemon .... yellow
spearmint, wintergreen .... green
anise .... black
orange........................... orange
sassafras .... light brown
lime............................. yellow green
raspberry........................ blue red
grape............................ purple

You will need to contact a confectionary supplier to obtain wooden sticks for lollipops and candied apples. Please don't substitute toothpicks or soft wood that can break or splinter in an unsuspecting mouth.

Lollipops and hard candies may be wrapped in waxed paper or in a plastic wrap, and then stored in tight containers. Large apothecary jars are good for this, especially if you want the tempting sweets to be seen.

HARD CANDY

confectioners' sugar, optional
3¾ cups sugar
1½ cups light corn syrup
1 cup water
1 teaspoon flavoring oil, or 1 tablespoon flavoring extract
5 to 6 drops food coloring

Place a 24 by 18-inch piece of heavy duty aluminum foil on a heat resistant surface. Lightly sprinkle with confectioners' sugar. Mix together sugar, corn syrup, and water in a heavy 3-quart saucepan. Cook over medium heat, stirring constantly, until mixture boils and sugar is dissolved. Boil without stirring until temperature reaches 310°F. on the candy thermometer (hard crack stage). Remove from heat. Add flavoring oil or extract and desired food coloring. Pour onto prepared foil. When the candy is cool and hard, break it into pieces. Store in layers between waxed paper in airtight container. Makes 2¼ pounds of candy.

MOSAIC CANDY

4 cups sugar
2 cups light corn syrup
1 cup water
1 tablespoon essence of peppermint, or desired flavoring
food coloring

Butter two jelly roll pans. Combine 2 cups sugar, 1 cup syrup, and ½ cup water in a heavy saucepan. Cook over medium heat, stirring constantly, until sugar is completely dissolved and mixture boils. Boil without stirring until temperature reaches 300°F. on the candy thermometer (hard crack stage). Stir in 1½ teaspoons of flavoring. Pour one-half of the mixture into another saucepan, which has been warmed. Color each half differently with food coloring. Pour each into a jelly roll pan. Break candy into pieces when cool. Arrange the pieces in a buttered jelly roll pan to make an artistic design. Combine remaining 2 cups sugar, 1 cup corn syrup, and ½ cup water into another batch of candy. Use the remaining flavoring, but omit any food coloring. Pour this mixture over the pieces of candy in the pan. Let cool. Break into pieces. Makes 2½ pounds of candy.

COFFEE DROPS

2 tablespoons instant coffee
1 tablespoon milk
2 cups sugar
⅔ cup light corn syrup
½ cup heavy cream
pinch salt

Butter a baking sheet. Dissolve instant coffee in milk and set aside. Combine sugar, corn syrup, cream, and salt in a heavy 3-quart saucepan. Stirring constantly, cook over medium-low heat until mixture comes to a boil. Cover and boil for 3 minutes. Remove cover and continue cooking without stirring until candy thermometer reaches 260°F. (hard ball stage). Stirring constantly, continue cooking until temperature reaches 300°F. (hard crack stage). Remove from heat. Gently stir in coffee mixture. To make coffee drops, carefully set saucepan in a skillet of boiling water over low heat. Drop mixture from a teaspoon onto the baking sheet, forming 1-inch patties, or, if desired, pour into a buttered 8-inch square pan. Cool the candy until almost set (about 10 minutes). Mark into squares or bars; then cool completely. Remove from pan and break apart. Wrap drops or bars individually and store in a tightly covered container. Makes about 1¼ pounds of candy.

CANDY VALENTINES

1 cup sugar
½ cup light corn syrup
¼ cup water
corn oil
¾ teaspoon peppermint extract
red food coloring

Mix together sugar, corn syrup, and water in a large saucepan. Cook over medium heat, stirring constantly, until mixture boils and sugar is dissolved. Boil without stirring until temperature reaches 295°F. (hard crack stage). Meanwhile brush heart-shaped cutters or molds with corn oil and place them on buttered cookie sheets. When the mixture has cooked, remove it from the heat and stir in the extract and food coloring. Pour immediately into the molds to a depth of ⅛-inch. Remove the forms when the candy is hard. Decorate with confectioners' sugar frosting or tiny cake decorating tubes. Makes about 12 regular-sized, cookie cutter hearts.

NOTE: Larger hearts may be shaped with heavy aluminum foil that has been turned up to form a shallow pan and oiled well.

Candy valentines.

LOLLIPOPS

4 cups sugar
2 cups light corn syrup
1 cup hot water
lemon, orange, or peppermint extract
food coloring
about 7 dozen lollipop skewers

Coat a marble slab, baking sheet, or piece of waxed paper with oil and arrange lollipop skewers 4 inches apart with the pointed ends facing in one direction.

In a large 4-quart saucepan, cook sugar, corn syrup, and water together until the candy thermometer reaches 270° F. (soft crack stage). Lower the heat and continue cooking to 310° F. (hard crack stage). Remove from heat and cool several minutes. Divide and add the flavoring and food coloring desired. Stir until well blended. When the temperature has lowered to 280° F. on the candy thermometer, pour tablespoonfuls of the syrup mixture onto the pointed ends of the wooden skewers. Let stand until cold and set. Makes about 80 lollipops.

BUTTERSCOTCH LOLLIPOPS

½ cup dark corn syrup
¼ cup butter
¾ cup sugar

Place 18 lollipop sticks 4 inches apart on greased baking sheet. Combine corn syrup, butter, and sugar in a heavy 1-quart saucepan. Cook over medium heat, stirring constantly, until sugar is dissolved and mixture comes to a boil. Continue cooking, stirring occasionally, until temperature reaches 270° F. (soft crack stage). Remove from heat. Drop candy mixture from a tablespoon over pointed end of each stick, forming a 2-inch disk. Cool. Makes 18 lollipops.

BUTTERSCOTCH DROPS

Prepare mixture as for BUTTERSCOTCH LOLLIPOPS. Drop by teaspoonfuls onto greased baking sheet. Makes about 48 drops, each 1¼ inches.

SPUN SUGAR

⅓ cup water
¼ cup light corn syrup
1 cup sugar

Combine water, corn syrup, and sugar in a small saucepan.

Bring to a boil over medium heat, stirring constantly. Boil, without stirring until temperature reaches 310°F. (hard crack stage). Remove from heat.

Meanwhile, grease the handles of 2 wooden spoons. Tape the spoons 12 inches apart flat to a tabletop, with handles extending out from the edge of the table. To protect the floor, spread newspapers in a wide area under the spoon handles. As soon as the syrup mixture is ready, dip a fork into the mixture. Shake rapidly back and forth over the greased protruding spoon handles, dipping fork and shaking until desired amount of spun sugar accumulates. (The faster you work the finer the strands will be.) Remove strands from spoons carefully. Repeat until all syrup mixture is used. Shape the spun sugar as desired. Plan to use this the same day, since spun sugar melts if it stands at room temperature.

CANDY APPLES

8 medium-sized red apples
8 wooden skewers
2 cups sugar
1 cup light corn syrup
½ cup water
¼ cup red cinnamon candies
10 drops red food coloring

Wash and dry apples; remove stems and insert skewers into stem ends. Combine sugar, corn syrup, and water in a heavy 2-quart saucepan. Stirring constantly, cook over medium heat until mixture boils and sugar is dissolved. Then cook without stirring until temperature reaches 250°F. on the candy thermometer (hard ball stage). Add cinnamon candies and continue cooking to 285°F. (soft crack stage). Remove from heat. Stir in red food coloring. Hold each apple by its skewer and quickly twirl in syrup, tilting pan to cover apple with syrup. Remove apple from syrup; allow excess to drip off, then twirl to spread syrup smoothly over apple. Place on lightly greased baking sheet to cool. Store in cool place. Makes 8 apples.

NOTE: If candy mixture cools too quickly, it may be reheated over low heat.

Cinnamon candy apples.

CINNAMON CANDY APPLES

8 medium-sized apples
8 wooden skewers
3 cups sugar
½ cup light corn syrup
½ cup water
1 drop oil of cinnamon
1 teaspoon red food coloring

Wash and dry apples; remove stems and insert skewers into stem ends. Combine sugar, corn syrup, and water in a heavy 2-quart saucepan. Stirring constantly, cook over medium heat until mixture boils and sugar is dissolved. Then cook without stirring until temperature reaches 250°F. on the candy thermometer (hard ball stage). Continue cooking without stirring to 285°F.

(soft crack stage). Remove from heat. Stir in oil of cinnamon and red food coloring, stirring just enough to mix through. Continue as for CANDY APPLES (page 89). Makes 8 apples.

CARAMEL APPLES

1 can sweetened condensed milk, 14-ounce size
1 cup sugar
½ cup light corn syrup
⅛ teaspoon salt
1 teaspoon vanilla
6 medium apples
6 wooden skewers

Lightly butter a baking sheet. Mix condensed milk, sugar, corn syrup, and salt in a heavy 2-quart saucepan. Cook over low heat, stirring constantly, until mixture comes to a boil and sugar is dissolved. Continue cooking over low heat, stirring constantly, until temperature reaches 232°F. on the candy thermometer, (thread or very soft ball stage). This may take as long as 30 minutes. Remove the mixture from heat; stir in vanilla and cool for 5 minutes. Insert wooden skewers in apples and dip in caramel mixture until well covered, tilting the pan as needed. Cool on the baking sheet. Makes 6 caramel apples.

La Belle Chocolatière.

Hershey candy labels.

Hershey electric car.   *Hershey candy label.*

Please mention THE BOOKLOVERS MAGAZINE *when you write to advertisers*

Peter's Swiss milk chocolate advertisement.

(Top) Lowney's advertisement; (bottom) milk trucks at Hershey chocolate factory.

A fashionable conditorei, old lithograph, undated.

Pralines, Brittles, and Buttercrunch

These are the crunchy candies! Choose any one of the recipes on the following pages if you want easy techniques and fast results. You'll have platefuls of irresistible sweets and have a good time too.

Pralines originated in France, but achieved their greatest and most lasting popularity in the pecan country in and around New Orleans. They are confections of nuts, usually pecans, cooked in a boiling syrup that was originally made with molasses. Later it was made with brown sugar or maple sugar. The secret of these patties is to beat the mixture until creamy and then to work quickly as you drop teaspoonfuls of the mixture onto a platter. Once dropped, allow the pralines to harden until firm without handling.

Brittles take careful watching and are best cooked in a heavy iron skillet—the old-fashioned black kind that has to be kept well oiled to prevent rust. Lightweight skillets just cannot spread the heat properly or prevent burning. If you let the sugar become too dark, it will have a decidedly burnt flavor and will have to be discarded. As you pour the brittle, be careful not to let it spatter on your skin. It is really very hot and can cause nasty burns.

A variation of brittle called sponge candy is made by adding a large quantity of baking soda at the last second. The candy foams up into an aerated mass. When cooled, the texture lacks the glasslike quality of brittle, but it has an interesting appearance of porousness.

Buttercrunch is probably the tastiest of this type of candy, as it is coated with chocolate and nuts or coconut. To set the chocolate quickly, refrigerate for a few minutes, and then remove to room temperature until hard.

Many of these candies are designed to be broken into odd shapes. Included in the group are butterscotch, English toffee, and a very old kind of vinegar candy. When they are hardened, crack into pieces with your hands, or if you wish, use the scraping spatula and hammer down lightly on the top of the handle to split the candy.

Store in a tightly covered container to retain crispness. If it is a see-through jar, it won't last long.

PRALINES

2 cups sugar
⅔ cup milk
⅓ cup dark corn syrup
¼ teaspoon salt
½ teaspoon vanilla
1 cup shelled pecan nuts

Combine sugar, milk, syrup, and salt in a medium saucepan. Cook over medium heat, stirring constantly, until sugar is dissolved. Cook without stirring until candy thermometer reaches 238°F. (soft ball stage). Remove from heat and cool to lukewarm (110°F.). Add vanilla. Then beat until mixture is thick and creamy. Stir in pecans. Drop from the tip of a spoon onto waxed paper. Shape with a spoon to form a circle and to spread pecans so that they are only one layer deep. Allow to remain undisturbed until the pralines are firm. Makes 1¼ pounds of candy.

CREAMY PRALINES

4 cups sugar
1 cup whipping cream
1 teaspoon grated orange rind
1 teaspoon vanilla
2 cups pecans
⅛ teaspoon salt

Combine 3 cups sugar, cream, and rind in a large heavy saucepan; cook to 236°F. on the candy thermometer (soft ball stage), stirring occasionally. Wash down the sides of the kettle with a pastry brush dipped in hot water. Remove from heat. Meanwhile, while this syrup is cooking, melt the remaining 1 cup of sugar in a heavy frying pan over very low heat, stirring constantly until it reaches a pale golden brown. (Do not cook the sugar too fast or too long as it will smoke and become bitter.) Slowly add the caramelized sugar to the cooked syrup, stirring with a long wooden spoon. Be very careful, as the candy foams up at this stage. The temperature of this mixture should be 236°F. on the candy thermometer; if not, heat slowly until the temperature is reached. Let cool to about 140°F. Then add vanilla, nuts, and salt. Beat with a heavy wooden spoon for about 5 or 6 minutes, until the candy begins to hold its shape and does not spread out when dropped from a teaspoon onto waxed paper. Place the pan in a skillet of very hot water. Pick up the candy with a teaspoon and form mounds on waxed paper, pushing the candy off the spoon with another teaspoon. Stir mixture in the pan occasionally. If it becomes too thick to shape, place mixture over very low heat for a few seconds until slightly loosened, but not too warm. Allow to cool before removing from waxed paper. Makes 40 medium-sized patties.

VANILLA PRALINES

2 cups sugar
⅔ cup milk
⅓ cup light corn syrup
¼ teaspoon salt
1 teaspoon vanilla
1 cup shelled pecan nuts

Combine sugar, milk, syrup, and salt in a medium saucepan. Cook over medium heat, stirring constantly, until sugar is dissolved. Cook without stirring until candy thermometer reaches 238°F. (soft ball stage). Remove from heat and cool to lukewarm (110°F.). Add vanilla. Then beat until mixture is thick and creamy. Stir in pecans. Drop from the tip of a spoon onto waxed paper. Shape with a spoon to form a circle and to spread pecans so that they are only one layer deep. Allow to remain undisturbed until the pralines are firm. Makes 1¼ pounds of candy.

MAPLE PRALINES

2½ cups maple sugar
⅛ teaspoon salt
¾ cup evaporated milk
2 tablespoons butter
2 cups pecan halves

Lightly butter a baking sheet. Mix maple sugar, salt, milk, and butter in a heavy saucepan. Cook, stirring constantly, over low heat, until sugar is dissolved. Add pecans and cook over medium heat to 234°F. (soft ball stage) on the candy thermometer, stirring constantly. Remove from heat; let cool for 5 minutes. Stir rapidly until mixture begins to thicken and coats pecans. Working quickly, drop by teaspoonfuls on baking sheet, forming patties. If candy stiffens and is slightly rough-looking before all patties are formed, soften and restore gloss by adding a little hot maple syrup. Makes about 48 candies.

SCOTCH KISSES

¾ cup sugar
⅔ cup brown sugar
¼ cup light corn syrup
⅔ cup water
6 tablespoons butter
1 teaspoon vanilla

Combine sugar, brown sugar, corn syrup, and water in a small saucepan. Cook over medium heat, stirring constantly until candy thermometer reaches 280°F. (soft crack stage). Add butter, stir in quickly and continue cooking to 287°F. Remove from heat. Add vanilla and stir only enough to mix. Drop from a teaspoon onto a greased baking sheet to form small rounds. Makes 36 to 48 pieces.

MAPLE BUTTERSCOTCH

1 cup sugar
¾ cup maple syrup
⅓ cup butter
½ cup water

Butter an 8-inch square pan. Combine all of the ingredients in a heavy saucepan. Bring to a boil and cook without stirring until the temperature reaches 285°F. (soft crack stage). Turn into the pan. Mark off the candy while it is still soft. Break it when it is cold. Makes about 60 pieces.

BUTTERSCOTCH

2 cups sugar
½ cup light corn syrup
½ cup butter
¾ cup water
½ teaspoon vanilla
½ teaspoon lemon juice

Butter an 8-inch square pan. Combine sugar, corn syrup, butter, and water in a deep heavy saucepan. Stir constantly, until candy thermometer reaches 278°F. (soft crack stage). Remove from heat, add vanilla and lemon juice, and pour into the pan. Cool. Mark into squares. Break or cut into squares when butterscotch is cold. Makes about 64 pieces.

ENGLISH TOFFEE

2 cups sugar
1½ cups butter
2 tablespoons water
2 cups blanched almonds

Butter a jelly roll pan. Combine sugar, butter, and water in a medium saucepan; cook over low heat, stirring constantly, until candy thermometer reaches 235°F. (soft ball stage). Stir in almonds and continue cooking without stirring until thermometer reaches 280°F. (soft crack stage). Pour into the jelly roll pan. Cool. Break into pieces. Makes about 1½ pounds of candy.

SIMPLE PEANUT BRITTLE

2 cups sugar
1 cup shelled peanuts

Butter a cookie sheet. Put sugar into a heavy skillet and cook over low heat until it slowly melts and turns into a clear reddish-brown colored liquid. Be careful not to let it burn. Meanwhile, arrange the peanuts in a single layer on the cookie sheet. Pour the melted sugar over them and allow it to harden. When cold and hard, break into pieces. Makes about 1 pound.

PEANUT BRITTLE

½ cup dark corn syrup
¼ cup molasses
¼ cup sugar
2 tablespoons butter
1 cup salted peanuts
⅛ teaspoon baking soda

Cook syrup, molasses, sugar, and butter until well blended. Stir in peanuts, and boil to 280°F. (soft crack stage). Stir in baking soda. Pour into buttered dish and cool. Remove candy from dish and break into irregular-shaped pieces. Makes about ½ pound of candy.

VINEGAR CANDY

3 cups sugar
½ cup water
⅔ cup vinegar

Butter a marble slab, cookie sheet, or other surface. Combine sugar, water, and vinegar in a saucepan. Bring to a boil, stirring constantly. Then boil without stirring until mixture reaches

Peanut brittle.

290°F. on the candy thermometer (hard crack stage). Pour at once onto prepared surface. Cool. Break into pieces. Makes about 1 pound.

CHOCOLATE COVERED SPONGE CANDY

1½ cups sugar
½ cup light corn syrup
¼ cup water
1 teaspoon baking soda
1 package semi-sweet chocolate chips, 6-ounce size
3 tablespoons water

Butter a cookie sheet. In a heavy 4-quart saucepan, stir together sugar, corn syrup, and water. Cook over medium heat, stirring constantly, until sugar is dissolved and mixture comes to a boil. Continue cooking without stirring until temperature reaches 300°F. (hard crack stage). Pour onto cookie sheet. Cool. Melt chocolate chips and 3 tablespoons water in a small saucepan over low heat. Spread over sponge candy. Cool until chocolate is set. Break into pieces. Makes 1¼ pounds of candy.

PEANUT SPONGE CANDY

3 cups sugar
1 cup light or dark corn syrup
½ cup water
3 cups salted peanuts
2 teaspoons baking soda

Butter two cookie sheets. In a heavy 4-quart saucepan, stir together sugar, corn syrup, and water. Cook over medium heat, stirring constantly, until sugar is dissolved and mixture comes to a boil. Continue cooking without stirring until candy thermometer reaches 280°F. (soft crack stage). Gradually stir in peanuts so mixture continues to boil. Cook, stirring frequently, until thermometer reaches 300°F. (hard crack stage). Remove from heat. Stir in baking soda quickly and gently. Immediately pour onto the cookie sheets. Cool. Break into pieces. Makes 2½ pounds of candy.

BUTTERCRUNCH

1 cup butter
1¼ cups sugar
2 tablespoons light corn syrup
2 tablespoons water
2 cups finely chopped almonds
2 packages semi-sweet chocolate chips, 6-ounce size

Butter a baking sheet. Combine butter, sugar, corn syrup, and water in a heavy saucepan. Place over medium heat, stirring constantly, until mixture boils. Reduce heat to low; continue cooking and stirring constantly until candy thermometer reaches 300°F. (hard crack stage). Remove from heat; stir in 1 cup of the chopped almonds. Quickly pour onto the baking sheet and spread about ¼-inch thick. Melt chocolate chips in top of a double boiler over hot, but not boiling, water. Spread one-half the melted chocolate over the top of the slightly warm candy; sprinkle with ½ cup chopped almonds; pat into chocolate. Carefully turn the candy over; spread with remaining melted chocolate. Sprinkle with remaining almonds and pat into chocolate. Cool completely or refrigerate briefly to set the chocolate. Break into irregular pieces. Makes about 1 pound of candy.

COCONUT BUTTERCRUNCH

1⅓ cups flaked coconut
1 cup butter
¾ cup sugar
1 package semi-sweet chocolate chips, 6-ounce size

Lightly butter a 9-inch square pan. Chop 1 cup of the coconut; then combine with butter and sugar in a saucepan. Cook over low heat, stirring occasionally, until mixture is light brown and a small amount will form a hard ball in cold water, 249°F. on the candy thermometer. Pour into the square pan. While still hot, top with chocolate chips. Let stand to melt chocolate; then spread chocolate evenly over the coconut mixture. Sprinkle with remaining coconut. Cool until firm; then break into pieces. Makes about 50 pieces.

Peanut sponge candy.

CHOCOLATE PEANUT CRUNCH

1½ cups peanuts
1½ cups sugar
1 package semi-sweet chocolate, 8-ounce size cut in small pieces
1 teaspoon butter

Butter a cookie sheet. Crush shelled peanuts with a rolling pin, or chop fine in a blender. Cook sugar in a heavy skillet until it melts to a butterscotch-colored syrup. Remove from heat. Stir in peanuts, chocolate, and butter, until well mixed. Pour onto the cookie sheet. Cool. When cold, break into pieces. Makes about 1 pound.

Jellied Candies
and Marshmallows

Maybe it is square to like square gumdrops and marsh-mallows, but a square is the easiest shape to make in a home kitchen. Homemade candies—no matter what the shape—have the same stick-to-your-teeth texture but none of the artificial ingredients usually stirred into commercial candies of the same type.

Of course, if a round form is important to you, you can fill a flat box with a one-inch layer of corn starch and shape holes in it to serve as molds. Then spoon the mixture into these holes and follow recipe directions to harden the candies. The corn starch may be used again and again for this purpose.

It is important to follow recipe directions, especially those that specify cooling and firming at room temperature. Forego the temptation to pop the pan into the refrigerator to speed up the process. Take the time needed to insure best results.

The basic recipes for orange and lemon gumdrops may be used for gumdrops of other flavors and colors. Just substitute ex-

tracts and food colorings in the list of ingredients. Follow the color and flavor suggestions on page 84, and your gumdrops will have a predictable taste.

Children will love making the Marshmallow Animals in this chapter. You may want to make shapes other than animals if the marshmallows are for adults. There is no need to worry about the waste of marshmallow scraps. Cut the scraps into tiny bits, add them to dairy sour cream, and use the mixture as a delicious dressing over mandarin oranges and coconut. It is sheer ambrosia!

PEPPERMINT CANDY JELLS

1 box dry fruit pectin
¾ cup water
½ teaspoon baking soda
1 cup sugar
1 cup light corn syrup
½ teaspoon peppermint extract
red and green food coloring
granulated sugar

Mix fruit pectin, water, and baking soda in a 2-quart saucepan. (Mixture will foam slightly.) Mix sugar and corn syrup in another saucepan. Place both saucepans over high heat. Cook both mixtures, stirring alternately, until foam has thinned from fruit pectin mixture and the sugar mixture is boiling rapidly—about 5 minutes.

Pour fruit pectin mixture in a slow steady stream into boiling sugar mixture, stirring constantly. Boil and stir for 1 minute longer. Remove from heat. Stir in extract. Divide and color each half, one with several drops of red food coloring, the other with several drops of green food coloring. Pour each into a 9 by 5-inch loaf pan. Let stand at room temperature until cool and firm—about 3 hours. Invert pans onto waxed paper that has been sprinkled with granulated sugar. Cut candy into squares with a knife that has been dipped in warm water; roll each square in sugar. Allow candy to stand a while; roll in sugar again to prevent stickiness. Let stand overnight, uncovered, at room temperature before packaging. Makes about 1 pound of candy.

CHOCOLATE GUMDROP SQUARES

3 envelopes unflavored gelatin, 1-ounce size
½ cup cold water
2 cups sugar
⅓ cup cocoa
⅔ cup water
1 teaspoon vanilla

Line the bottom of an 8-inch square pan with waxed paper. Soften gelatin in ½ cup cold water. Combine sugar, cocoa, and ⅔ cup water in a heavy saucepan; cook, stirring constantly, until the sugar is dissolved. Stir in gelatin and bring mixture to a boil. Cook over low heat for 15 minutes, without stirring, until candy thermometer reaches 220°F. Remove from the heat and stir in vanilla. Pour into the pan. Chill until firm. Invert onto a well-sugared surface. Carefully peel off the waxed paper. Cut into 1-inch squares and roll each in granulated sugar. Makes 64 candies.

ARMENIAN GUMDROPS

3 cups sugar
3 tablespoons corn starch
¼ teaspoon salt
1 cup water
3 envelopes unflavored gelatin, 1-ounce size
¾ cup cold water
1¼ cups chopped nuts
2 tablespoons lemon juice
1 teaspoon vanilla
½ teaspoon almond extract
½ teaspoon finely grated lemon rind
1 drop yellow food coloring
sifted confectioners' sugar

Combine sugar, corn starch, and salt in a medium saucepan. Gradually stir in 1 cup water. Bring to a boil, stirring constantly. Boil gently, stirring occasionally, until temperature reaches 240°F. on the candy thermometer (soft ball stage). Sprinkle gelatin over cold water. Let soften for 5 minutes. Add to hot mixture and stir until gelatin is completely dissolved. Stir in nuts, lemon

Armenian gumdrops.

juice, vanilla, almond extract, grated lemon rind, and food coloring. Pour mixture into a 9-inch square pan. Chill until stiff. Cut into squares and dust on all sides with confectioners' sugar. Makes about 64 squares.

TURKISH DELIGHT

8 envelopes unflavored gelatin, 1-ounce size
2 cups sugar
1 cup water
⅛ teaspoon salt
½ cup undiluted frozen concentrated orange juice
1 cup finely chopped nuts
confectioners' sugar

Stir gelatin and sugar together in a large saucepan. Add water and salt. Cook over low heat, stirring constantly, until gelatin and sugar are dissolved. Then let simmer for 20 minutes, stirring occasionally. Remove from heat; add concentrated orange juice and mix well. Chill, stirring occasionally, until slightly thickened. Stir in chopped nuts. Rinse an 8-inch square pan with cold water; turn gelatin mixture into pan and chill until firm. Unmold onto a board dusted with confectioners' sugar. Cut into 1-inch squares. Roll in confectioners' sugar to coat all sides. Makes 64 squares.

ORANGE GUMDROPS

1 bottle liquid pectin, 6-ounce size
¼ teaspoon baking soda
¾ cup sugar
¾ cup light corn syrup
1½ teaspoons orange extract
1 teaspoon grated orange rind
4 drops yellow food coloring
2 drops red food coloring
sugar

Combine pectin and baking soda in a 1-quart saucepan (pectin will foam). Combine ¾ cup sugar and corn syrup in a 2-quart saucepan. Cook each mixture at the same time over high heat, stirring frequently, until foam disappears from pectin mixture and sugar mixture comes to a rapid boil—3 to 5 minutes. Continue stirring as you pour the pectin mixture into the boiling sugar mixture in a slow steady stream. Boil for 1 minute, stirring constantly. Remove from heat; add orange extract, orange rind, and food colorings. Immediately pour into an 8-inch square pan. Let stand at room temperature until firm and cool—about 2 hours. Cut into ½-inch cubes; roll in sugar. Store in refrigerator. Makes about 60 pieces of candy.

LEMON GUMDROPS

1 bottle liquid pectin, 6-ounce size
¼ teaspoon baking soda

¾ cup sugar
¾ cup light corn syrup
1½ teaspoons lemon extract
1 teaspoon grated lemon rind
3 drops yellow food coloring
sugar

Combine pectin and baking soda in a 1-quart saucepan. Combine ¾ cup sugar and corn syrup in a 2-quart saucepan. Cook each mixture at the same time over high heat, stirring frequently, until foam disappears from pectin mixture and sugar mixture comes to a rapid boil—3 to 5 minutes. Continue stirring as you pour the pectin mixture into the boiling sugar mixture in a slow steady stream. Boil for 1 minute, stirring constantly. Remove from heat; add lemon extract, lemon rind, and food coloring. Immediately pour into an 8-inch square pan. Let stand at room temperature until firm and cool—about 2 hours. Cut into ½-inch cubes; roll in sugar. Store in refrigerator. Makes about 60 pieces of candy.

APPLE MINT JELLIES

1½ cups applesauce
1½ cups sugar
½ cup light corn syrup
2 envelopes unflavored gelatin, 1-ounce size
½ cup cold water
2 tablespoons lemon juice
1 teaspoon mint extract
green food coloring, about 6 drops
½ cup slivered blanched almonds
fine granulated sugar

Line an 8-inch square baking pan with foil. Stir together, over medium heat, applesauce, sugar, and corn syrup in a 3-quart saucepan. Bring to a full rolling boil, stirring constantly, and boil 20 minutes or until mixture is reduced to 2 cups. Sprinkle gelatin over cold water to soften. Remove applesauce mixture from heat; stir in softened gelatin until dissolved. Add lemon juice, mint extract, food coloring, and almonds, mixing thoroughly. Pour into the pan. Chill until firm—4 hours or overnight. Lift candy in the foil to a cutting surface. Cut foil from sides of candy and lay flat.

Cut candy into 1-by-½-inch pieces. Roll in fine sugar. Store uncovered in refrigerator. Makes about 120 pieces of candy.

APPLE CANDY

2 cups cooked and sieved tart apples
2 cups sugar
⅛ teaspoon salt
3 tablespoons unflavored gelatin
6 tablespoons cold water
1 cup chopped walnuts
4 teaspoons lemon juice
confectioners' sugar

Butter a shallow pan. To obtain cooked sieved tart apples, wash about 7 apples, then core and cut unpeeled into small pieces. Cook in just enough water to prevent their sticking to the pan. When apples are soft, put through a sieve and measure. Combine cooked apples, sugar, and salt. Cook until mixture becomes thick, stirring constantly to prevent scorching. Soak the gelatin in the cold water to soften it; add to the hot apple mixture, stirring until the gelatin dissolves. Remove from heat; add nuts and lemon juice. Pour into the pan. Cool, then refrigerate. When candy has set, cut into squares, and roll in confectioners' sugar. Makes about 64 pieces.

JELLY BONBONS

1 cup currant or apple jelly
1 envelope unflavored gelatin, 1-ounce size
½ cup water
1 cup semi-sweet chocolate chips

Butter an 8-inch square pan. Melt jelly over hot water in a double boiler over medium heat. Meanwhile, soften gelatin in ½ cup water; add to jelly and stir well. Pour into the pan. Chill until very firm. Cut into ½-inch cubes. Melt chocolate chips over hot water in a double boiler; cool to lukewarm. Then dip jelly cubes into the chocolate. Place on racks to dry. Makes 128 one-half-inch cubes or 64 one-inch cubes.

PLAIN MARSHMALLOWS

1 envelope plain gelatin
⅓ cup cold water
½ cup sugar
⅔ cup light corn syrup
½ teaspoon vanilla
¼ cup corn starch
¼ cup fine granulated sugar

Soften gelatin in cold water in a small saucepan or top of double boiler. Place pan over boiling water and stir until gelatin is dissolved. Add sugar and stir until sugar is dissolved. Pour corn syrup into a large bowl of an electric mixer. Add the vanilla and the gelatin and sugar mixture. Beat about 15 minutes or until the mixture becomes thick and of a marshmallow-like consistency. Combine corn starch and fine granulated sugar; use about one-third of the mixture to cover the bottom of a 7 by 10 by 1½-inch pan completely. Pour marshmallow into pan and smooth the top with a knife. Let it stand in a cool place (not in the refrigerator) until well set—about 1 hour. Remove from the pan by loosening around edges with a knife; invert over a board sprinkled lightly with another one-third of the corn starch mixture. Cut into squares with a sharp knife that has been moistened with cold water. Roll in the remaining corn starch mixture. Makes about 1 pound.

TOASTED COCONUT MARSHMALLOWS

Butter sides and bottom of a pan. Chop 2 cups shredded coconut very fine and place in a shallow baking pan; bake in a 350°F. oven, stirring occasionally until coconut is toasted to a delicate brown. Sprinkle the buttered pan with part of toasted coconut. Prepare PLAIN MARSHMALLOWS (above) as directed, omitting corn starch and granulated sugar mixture. Pour into prepared pan. Smooth the top with a knife; sprinkle top with toasted coconut. When set, remove from pan and cut as directed. Roll cut sides in remaining toasted coconut. Makes about 1 pound.

CHOCOLATE MARSHMALLOWS

Follow recipe for PLAIN MARSHMALLOWS (page 115). When beating is half complete (about 7 minutes), continue beating as you add 3 tablespoons cocoa and ½ teaspoon salt. Beat until the mixture becomes thick and of a marshmallow-like consistency. Finish the recipe. Makes about 1 pound.

CHOCOLATE COVERED MARSHMALLOWS

1 milk chocolate bar, 7½-ounce size
2 tablespoons shortening
35 large marshmallows
toothpicks
chopped peanuts (for garnish)
or
flaked coconut (for garnish)

Line a cookie sheet with waxed paper. Melt the milk chocolate and shortening in the top of a double boiler over hot, but not boiling, water. Keep warm. Place toothpicks in the center of each marshmallow and dip into melted chocolate, covering completely. Roll in desired garnish of chopped peanuts or flaked coconut and place on the cookie sheet. Chill 15 minutes. Serve cold. Makes 35 pieces.

MARSHMALLOW ANIMALS

3 envelopes unflavored gelatin, 1-ounce size
1¼ cups water
2 cups sugar
2 tablespoons light corn syrup
1 teaspoon almond extract
1 cup icy cold evaporated milk
2 tablespoons lemon juice
shredded coconut

Grease a 9 by 13-inch baking pan. In a large mixing bowl, sprinkle gelatin on ½ cup of the water to soften. In a saucepan, mix together the remaining ¾ cup water, sugar, and corn syrup; cook over medium heat, stirring constantly, until it reaches a rolling

Marshmallow animals.

boil. Cook for 5 minutes without stirring. Pour over the softened gelatin; stir until gelatin is dissolved. Add almond extract. Cool at room temperature to a thick syrup consistency, about 1 hour, stirring occasionally. Meanwhile, chill evaporated milk by pouring into a freezer tray; when ice crystals form around the edges, turn into a chilled bowl and beat with electric mixer at high speed until soft peaks are formed, about 2 minutes. Gradually add 2 tablespoons lemon juice and continue whipping about 2 minutes. Add whipped mixture to cooled syrup mixture, and beat until smooth. Turn into the baking pan. Chill about 1 hour. Cut with cookie cutters; lightly toss in coconut. Makes 10 to 20 candies, depending on the size of cookie cutters.

NOTE: Melt trimmings in the top half of a double boiler, over rapidly boiling water. Chill until mixture mounds slightly when dropped from a spoon. Beat until smooth. Turn into a greased 8-inch square baking pan. Proceed with cookie cutters.

Fruit Candies

Nutritious candies—with less sugar than ordinary candies—may be made with fruit, a natural ingredient. Dried fruits such as apricots, dates, prunes, and figs are the basis of delicious sweets. Stuff them, or let them be the "stuffing" after they have been rolled in coconut or sugar, or perhaps hand-dipped in tempered chocolate.

Fresh fruit may be dipped in chocolate the way Thomas Kron, a famous New York chocolatier, does it. His tiny shop is always crowded with customers buying chocolate covered strawberries and orange sections. Only firm plump strawberries with green stems intact are used. They are dipped halfway, so some of the strawberry and all of the stem still show, and set aside to harden. The oranges are peeled, trimmed of excess white flesh, and then divided into segments. Each segment is completely covered with chocolate, using the method described in Chapter 4 for hand-dipping chocolate centers. These are incredible delicacies; but they spoil rapidly, so use them up within one or two days.

Do not overlook the economical advantage of using the discarded orange peels to prepare candied citrus peels, following the recipe in this chapter. You may use the same recipe if you have a whim to make candied violets or rose petals for use as cake decorations. Would you believe—they're edible too!

Pitted prunes and tiny dried apricots also are delicious dipped in chocolate. They may be kept for longer periods of time than their fresh fruit counterparts.

Other recipes in this chapter are simple to prepare and well worth the effort as you turn everyday pantry products into tender confections.

CHOCOLATE CHERRY CORDIALS

1 cup semi-sweet chocolate chips
1 cup milk chocolate chips
2 teaspoons shortening
¼ cup butter
2 cups confectioners' sugar
1 tablespoon milk
½ teaspoon vanilla
⅛ teaspoon almond extract .
4 dozen maraschino cherries, drained

Place both kinds of chocolate chips into the top of a double boiler; add shortening and melt over hot water. Cool to 78°F. Cream butter with confectioners' sugar. Add milk, vanilla, and almond extract. (If mixture is too sticky, add up to ¼ cup additional confectioners' sugar.) Mold a small amount of this mixture around each cherry, covering completely. Cover and chill. When ready to dip into chocolate coating, heat cooled chocolate to 88°F. over warm water; maintain temperature while dipping. Drop each center, one at a time, into chocolate; roll to coat completely and remove with a fork. Draw fork across the rim of the pan to remove excess chocolate. Drop from fork, upside down onto waxed paper, swirling a thread of chocolate from fork across top for a decorative touch. Chill 20 minutes. Store in a cool place for 1 or 2 days to allow cherry covering to liquefy and form the "cordial." Makes 4 dozen candies.

CHOCOLATE FRUIT DROPS

1 6-ounce package semi-sweet chocolate chips
1 cup chopped pitted prunes
1 cup miniature marshmallows

Grease a cookie sheet. Melt chocolate chips in the top of a double boiler over hot water. Remove from heat and stir in prunes and marshmallows. Drop by teaspoonfuls on cookie sheet. Cool at room temperature until firm. Makes 24 candies.

Your
Today?

CALIFORNIA
SUN-MAID
SEEDLESS
RAISINS
5¢.

Five Cents Worth
of *Healthfulness*

SUN-MAID
SEEDLESS
RAISINS

5¢.

PEANUT BUTTER PRUNE BALLS

½ pound pitted prunes
½ cup chunk-style peanut butter
¼ cup confectioners' sugar
granulated sugar

Soak prunes in cold water for 30 minutes. Drain and dry. Grind prunes twice through a food grinder. Combine ground prunes, peanut butter, and confectioners' sugar. Mix well. Form into 1-inch balls and roll in granulated sugar. Store in tightly covered container. Makes about ¾ pound of candy.

CHEWY GINGER ROLL

1 cup raisins
1 cup chopped nuts
1 cup miniature marshmallows
1 cup broken gingersnaps
⅓ cup dark corn syrup
3 tablespoons butter
1½ tablespoons orange juice
2¼ cups confectioners' sugar
⅓ cup instant nonfat dry milk
shredded coconut (optional)

Combine raisins, nuts, marshmallows, and gingersnap pieces in a large bowl; set aside. Combine corn syrup, butter, and orange juice in a saucepan. Bring to a boil, then reduce heat to low. Combine confectioners' sugar and dry milk. Stir into syrup mixture, stirring until dissolved. Pour over raisin mixture in bowl. Toss to coat evenly. Chill slightly, then shape into a roll. Chill until firm enough to cut, about 1 hour. Roll in coconut, if desired. Slice. Makes about 1½ pounds of candy.

DATE NUT ROLL

3 cups sugar
1 cup light cream
½ cup dark corn syrup
1 cup chopped dates

1 cup chopped nuts
1 teaspoon almond extract

Lightly grease a large piece of aluminum foil. Combine sugar, light cream, and corn syrup in a saucepan. Cook over medium heat, stirring constantly, until sugar dissolves; then cook without stirring until temperature reaches 248°F. on the candy thermometer (hard ball stage). Stir in dates and nuts. Cook 3 minutes. Remove from heat; stir in almond extract. Let cool to about 150°F. Beat until mixture is very stiff, at least 5 minutes. Shape into a long roll, about 1½-inches in diameter, in the aluminum foil. (Candy will be soft.) Chill thoroughly, and when firm, cut into ¼-inch slices. Makes about 6 dozen pieces.

RAISIN CLUSTERS

1 6-ounce package semi-sweet chocolate chips
¼ cup light corn syrup
1½ teaspoons vanilla
2 tablespoons confectioners' sugar
2 cups raisins

Grease a cookie sheet. Combine chocolate chips and corn syrup in the top of a double boiler. Place over boiling water and stir until chocolate is melted. Mix in vanilla and confectioners' sugar. Mix in rasins. Drop by teaspoonfuls onto the cookie sheet. Chill until firm. Makes about 3 dozen.

CANDIED PRUNES

1 cup sugar
½ cup apple juice
1 12-ounce package pitted prunes
miniature marshmallows
red and green candied cherries
golden raisins
whole blanched almonds

Bring sugar and apple juice to a boil, stirring constantly. Add pitted prunes and simmer for 20 minutes. Remove prunes with a slotted spoon and cool on a rack. Fill cavities of prunes with marshmallows, candied cherries, golden raisins, and almonds. Roll in granulated sugar. Makes about 1 pound of candied prunes.

CANDIED DRIED FRUIT

36 large prunes, figs, or apricot halves
1 cup sugar
½ cup water
¼ cup light corn syrup
dash salt
confectioners' sugar

Put dried fruit into a strainer. Steam over boiling water for about 10 minutes to soften slightly. Cool. Combine sugar, water, corn syrup, and salt in a heavy saucepan. Cook over medium heat, stirring constantly, until sugar is dissolved. Then, cook without stirring, until temperature reaches 238°F. on the candy thermometer (soft ball stage). Place pan in cold water immediately to stop boiling, then set over hot water to keep syrup from thickening. Dip fruit in syrup, holding each piece with a cake tester or two-tined fork. Place on wire rack over waxed paper. Cool. Roll in confectioners' sugar. Makes 36 pieces.

APRICOT COCONUT BALLS

½ cup light corn syrup
2 tablespoons butter
1 tablespoon water
½ teaspoon vanilla
¼ teaspoon almond extract
⅔ cup instant nonfat dry milk
2 cups dried apricots, finely chopped or ground
2 cups flaked coconut, finely cut
confectioners' sugar (optional)

Blend corn syrup and butter. Stir in water, vanilla, almond extract, and nonfat dry milk. Combine apricots and coconut. Add to syrup mixture and knead until well blended. Shape into 1-inch balls. Dust with confectioners' sugar, if desired. Chill. Makes about 1½ pounds of candy.

DRIED FRUIT BALLS

1 cup seedless raisins
1 cup pitted prunes
1 cup figs
½ cup chopped walnuts
confectioners' sugar

Grind raisins, prunes, and figs through the fine blade of a food grinder. Mix well. Add chopped nuts. Refrigerate. Shape mixture into 1-inch balls. Roll in confectioners' sugar. Makes about 3 dozen balls.

CANDIED FRUIT SQUARES

⅓ cup butter
⅓ cup light corn syrup
1 teaspoon rum or rum extract
½ teaspoon salt
1 pound confectioners' sugar, sifted
½ cup finely chopped mixed candied fruit

Blend butter with corn syrup, rum, and salt in a large mixing bowl. Add confectioners' sugar all at once and mix in, first with a spoon, then kneading with hands. Add candied fruit. Roll out to ½-inch thickness. Cut into squares. Makes about 1½ pounds of candy.

CANDIED CITRUS PEEL

2 grapefruit
3 large navel oranges
1½ cups water
4 cups sugar

Trim peels away from fruit, setting fruit aside for another purpose. Trim all white flesh from the insides of the peels. Cut peels into ¼-inch-wide strips; place in a saucepan and cover with water. Bring to a boil and sustain boiling action for about 15 minutes. Drain. Cover with water again and repeat the boiling process; drain again. Combine 1½ cups water and 3 of the cups of sugar; pour over the drained cooked peel. Cook again, over high heat, stirring until the mixture boils. Continue boiling until candy thermometer reaches 238°F., about 20 minutes, stirring occasionally. Remove peel from syrup with a slotted spoon and spread on a rack or paper towel to dry. Stir peel in a bowl with ½ cup of sugar until well coated; then spread again to dry for several hours. Again, stir peel in a bowl with the remaining ½ cup of sugar, and store in a tightly covered container. Makes about 1 pound of candy.

STUFFED DATES

1 recipe BASIC UNCOOKED FONDANT
1¾ pounds pitted dates
sugar

Prepare fondant as directed. Shape into very small finger-shaped rolls and stuff into pitted dates. Roll in granulated sugar. Makes about 3 pounds of candy.

FRUIT NUGGETS

1 pound uncooked dried fruit
rind of 1 orange
orange juice
½ cup finely chopped nuts

Put dried fruit and orange rind through a food chopper, using a fine blade. Moisten with just enough orange juice to hold the mixture together. Form into 1-inch balls. Roll in chopped nuts. Makes about 2 dozen balls.

FRUIT-NUT CHEWS

1 cup dried apricots
1 cup dried stemmed figs or pitted dates
1 cup seeded muscat raisins
½ cup shelled almonds or walnuts, chopped
½ cup light or dark corn syrup
⅛ teaspoon salt
finely chopped coconut

Fruit nut chews.

Wash fruit and drain thoroughly. Grind fruit in a food chopper, using the coarse blade. Mix and grind once more. Combine fruit, nuts, corn syrup, and salt in the top part of a double boiler; cook over boiling water, until fruit softens slightly and mixture can be stirred until well blended. Heat until soft, mixing thoroughly. Pour into a shallow pan lined with waxed paper, and let harden overnight. Cut into desired shapes and roll in finely chopped coconut. To store, wrap in waxed paper and keep in a cool place. Makes about 2 pounds.

NOTE: Instead of rolling in coconut, chews may be rolled in granulated sugar.

Nut Candies

What would a circus or a baseball game be without the aroma of hot roasted peanuts? And who can forget the warmth of roasting chestnuts as they come from the fire? Travelers in the South can add the delights of peanut confections to this list of nutty nostalgia, as they follow the Stuckey signs to sweet rewards.

Nuts are nature's most generous offerings to the inveterate nibbler. Peanuts especially are high in protein and, therefore, are a valuable nutritional bonus. All kinds of nuts lend themselves to candymaking, whether they are pecan or walnut halves hugging a ball of fondant, mixed nuts covered with chocolate and formed into mounds, or ground almonds mixed with sugar and held together with corn syrup to form pretty candies of marzipan. Ground, chopped, glacéed, toasted, or roasted—here is a chapter full of interesting ideas for serving the nuts in your life.

If the recipe calls for unsalted nuts, and the ones you planned to use are full of salt, do not wash them. Just put them in a strainer with large holes and shake them back and forth over the sink until most of the salt has fallen away.

When a recipe calls for ground nuts, use your electric blender to do the job. Grind a few nuts at a time for best results, otherwise some will be overground almost into a paste while the rest may be chopped too coarsely. If you do not own a blender, rely on a good hand-operated nut chopper. Of course, both of these can be used to chop nuts too, but the blender will need careful attention to be sure that the end result is not too fine; just a flick on and off of the blender switch is usually enough to chop nuts.

To remove skins from nuts, pour boiling water over them, and then plunge them immediately into icy water. The skins will slip off with ease. Drain and dry well before using the nuts in a recipe.

Older generations will adore the Rocky Road candies, as they recall years gone by when this candy was a special treat. Younger generations will be telling their grandchildren about your candy kitchen fifty years from now. Reason enough to close the generation gap!

ROCKY ROAD CANDY

½ pound marshmallows
1 cup walnuts, broken into pieces
1 pound milk chocolate

Cut the marshmallows into small pieces with kitchen scissors, which must be moistened frequently in cold water. Sprinkle the marshmallows and nuts evenly over the bottom of a buttered 8-inch square pan. Slowly melt the chocolate in the top of a double boiler (it will take about an hour) over lukewarm water. If the water is too hot, the candy will become an unattractive white. Pour the melted chocolate over the marshmallows and nuts. When cool, mark and cut into squares. Makes about 48 pieces.

FRUITED ROCKY ROAD CANDY

6 large marshmallows, quartered
8 red candied cherries, halved
⅓ cup walnuts, broken into pieces
¼ cup raisins or chopped dates
2 milk chocolate bars, 7½-ounce size

½ *cup ground walnuts*
¾ *teaspoon grated orange peel, optional*

Lightly butter a 9-inch square pan. Arrange marshmallows, cherries, broken walnuts, and raisins or dates on bottom of pan. Melt chocolate bars in top of a double boiler over warm water; stir in ground walnuts and orange peel. Pour over ingredients in pan, using a spatula or knife to smooth chocolate carefully over entire surface. Tap pan firmly on counter several times to settle chocolate. Cover; chill several hours or until set. Remove from refrigerator about 20 minutes before cutting; cut into squares and refrigerate until serving time. Makes about 36 pieces.

Rocky Road candy.

RUM BALLS

5 cups finely crushed vanilla cookies
1 cup chopped pecans
1 cup confectioners' sugar
½ cup rum
¼ cup light corn syrup
2 tablespoons cocoa
confectioners' sugar

Combine cookie crumbs, pecans, 1 cup confectioners' sugar, rum, corn syrup, and cocoa. Dust your hands with confectioners' sugar and shape the mixture into 1-inch balls. Roll balls in confectioners' sugar. Store in tightly covered container for several days to mellow. Makes about 4 dozen balls.

CHOCOLATE NUT MOUNDS

1 one-pound bar pure chocolate
½ teaspoon orange extract
2 cups mixed nuts

Melt chocolate in a double boiler over hot water at about 110° to 120°F. Temper it, as described in Chapter 4, until a dab of chocolate tested under your lower lip feels cold to the touch. Work in orange extract. If nuts are salted, shake them in a large-holed strainer to remove most of the salt. Then take a few nuts at a time and with the fingers of one hand, stir them into a corner of the tempered chocolate until they are completely covered. Work them into a small mass and, turning your hand upside down, push the mass off your fingers with your thumb onto a piece of waxed paper. Repeat this action until all the chocolate and nuts have been worked into mounds. If the chocolate hardens before you are finished, reheat it as before and temper to the right condition again before proceeding. Makes about 2 pounds of candy.

DATE-NUT LOGS

1 tablespoon butter
¼ cup light corn syrup
½ teaspoon vanilla
3 tablespoons instant nonfat dry milk

¼ *teaspoon salt*
2 *cups sifted confectioners' sugar*
1 *cup dates, finely cut*
1 *cup chopped nuts*

Blend butter and corn syrup; stir in vanilla. Combine nonfat dry milk, salt, and confectioners' sugar; add to corn syrup mixture. Add dates. Stir and knead until thoroughly mixed. Form into small rolls. Dip each roll into chopped nuts. Makes about 1¼ pounds of candy.

NUTTY MOCHA BALLS

6 *squares semi-sweet chocolate, 1-ounce size*
¼ *cup light corn syrup*
2 *cups confectioners' sugar*
2 *tablespoons instant coffee powder*
½ *cup hot milk*
1 *teaspoon vanilla*
1⅜ *cups graham cracker crumbs*
1 *cup chopped walnuts*
½ *cup finely chopped walnuts*

Melt chocolate in the top of a double boiler over hot water. Add corn syrup and sugar, mixing well. Stir coffee powder into milk and stir into chocolate mixture. Add vanilla, graham cracker crumbs, and chopped walnuts, mixing well. Chill about 1 hour, or until firm enough to handle. Roll into 1-inch balls. Roll balls in finely chopped walnuts. Cover and store in refrigerator. Makes about 40 balls.

PEANUT BUTTER COCONUT ROLL

¼ *cup creamy peanut butter*
¼ *cup dark corn syrup*
2 *teaspoons water*
2 *cups sifted confectioners' sugar*
¼ *cup instant nonfat dry milk*
¼ *teaspoon salt*
1 *cup flaked coconut, finely cut*

Blend peanut butter and corn syrup together; stir in water. Combine confectioners' sugar, nonfat dry milk and salt; mix into peanut butter mixture. Add coconut. Knead until well blended. Shape into a roll and wrap in waxed paper. Chill until firm—several hours or overnight. Cut into ¼-inch slices with a sharp knife. Makes about ¾ pound of candy.

SPICED WALNUTS

1 cup sugar
⅓ cup water
¼ cup light corn syrup
¼ teaspoon cinnamon
⅛ teaspoon nutmeg
¼ teaspoon salt
2 cups shelled walnuts

Grease a baking sheet. Mix together sugar, water, and corn syrup in a 2-quart saucepan. Cook over medium heat, stirring constantly, until sugar is dissolved and mixture comes to a boil. Continue cooking, stirring occasionally, until temperature reaches 235°F. on the candy thermometer (soft ball stage). Remove from heat. Add cinnamon, nutmeg, salt, and walnuts. Stir until mixture begins to thicken and turns white. Pour onto the baking sheet and separate nuts into clusters. Cool and store in an airtight container. Makes about 1 pound.

CANDIED WALNUTS

1 cup sugar
⅓ cup water
¼ cup light corn syrup
1 teaspoon rum extract
¼ teaspoon salt
2 cups shelled walnuts

Grease a baking sheet. Mix together sugar, water, and corn syrup in a 2-quart saucepan. Cook over medium heat, stirring constantly, until sugar is dissolved and mixture comes to a boil. Continue cooking, stirring occasionally, until temperature reaches 235°F. on the candy thermometer (soft ball stage). Remove from heat. Add rum extract, salt, and walnuts. Stir until mixture begins to thicken and turns white. Pour onto baking sheet and separate nuts into clusters. Cool and store in an airtight container. Makes about 1 pound.

MINTED WALNUTS

1 cup sugar
½ cup water
¼ cup light corn syrup
10 marshmallows
1 teaspoon peppermint extract
10 drops green food coloring
3 cups walnut halves

Mix sugar, water, and corn syrup in a heavy 2-quart saucepan. Bring to a boil over medium heat, stirring constantly. Cook until candy thermometer reaches 238°F. (soft ball stage). Remove from heat. Mix in marshmallows, peppermint, and food coloring; stir until marshmallows are melted. Add nuts and stir until well coated. Turn onto waxed paper. Separate nuts while still warm. Makes 1¼ pounds.

Minted walnuts.

BUTTERSCOTCH PECANS

¾ cup light brown sugar
¼ cup dark corn syrup
2 tablespoons light cream
1 tablespoon water
2 tablespoons butter
1½ cups broken pecans

Grease a cookie sheet. Combine brown sugar, corn syrup, cream, and water in a saucepan. Bring to a boil over medium heat, stirring constantly. Continue cooking, stirring occasionally, until temperature reaches 260°F. on the candy thermometer (hard ball stage). Add butter. Continue cooking, stirring constantly, until temperature reaches 280°F. (soft crack stage). Stir in nuts, coating evenly. Immediately spread out on the cookie sheet. Break apart when cold. Makes 1 pound.

GLACE NUTS

1½ cups sugar
½ cup light corn syrup
½ cup water
½ teaspoon salt
3 cups shelled nuts
2 tablespoons butter
1 teaspoon vanilla

Grease a square pan, and also a large, shallow pan. Combine sugar, corn syrup, water, and salt in a heavy saucepan. Cook over low heat, stirring constantly, until sugar is dissolved. Then cook over medium heat, without stirring, until mixture reaches 300°F. on the candy thermometer (hard crack stage). Meanwhile, spread nuts in a shallow pan and heat in a 350°F. oven for 10 minutes. Reduce heat under syrup mixture to very low; add nuts, butter, and vanilla. Stir just until nuts are coated and butter is melted. Remove from heat. Turn out into a large, coarse sieve set over the square pan. Let excess syrup drain off for about 1 minute. Spread out nuts in the large, shallow pan, using forks to separate nuts. Cool excess syrup mixture, then break into pieces and serve as hard candy. Makes 3 cups of nuts and hard candy.

WALNUT DROPS

1 cup brown sugar
½ cup granulated sugar
¼ cup light corn syrup
½ cup light cream
1 tablespoon butter
1 teaspoon vanilla
1½ cups chopped walnuts

Combine sugars, corn syrup, and cream in a saucepan. Cook over very low heat, stirring constantly, until candy thermometer reaches 238°F. (soft ball stage). Mixture will curdle if cooked too rapidly and should take about 35 minutes to this point. Remove from heat; add butter and vanilla. Beat until well blended—about 1 minute. Add chopped walnuts; stir until coated. Quickly drop by spoonfuls onto waxed paper. When cold and set, remove from paper. Makes about 30 pieces of candy.

MARZIPAN CHOCOLATE KISSES

¾ cup slivered almonds
½ cup confectioners' sugar
5 teaspoons light corn syrup
1 teaspoon almond extract
¼ teaspoon red food coloring
24 milk chocolate kisses, unwrapped
granulated sugar

Put slivered almonds in electric blender container; cover and blend at high speed until very finely chopped. Pour into mixing bowl and combine with confectioners' sugar. Combine corn syrup, almond extract, and food color; drizzle into almond mixture and stir until slightly blended. Mix with hands until mixture clings together. Press about 1 teaspoon of the marzipan mixture around a chocolate kiss, maintaining the kiss shape. Roll in granulated sugar. Store in airtight container. Makes 24 kisses.

NOTE: For variety, omit the almond extract and red food coloring and substitute one of the following:

Orange   ¾ teaspoon orange extract, 7 drops red and 14 drops yellow food color.

Lemon   ¾ teaspoon lemon extract and ¼ teaspoon yellow food color.

Rum   ¾ teaspoon rum extract and ¼ teaspoon green food color.

MARZIPAN CANDY

3 tablespoons light corn syrup
¼ teaspoon vanilla
¼ teaspoon almond extract
dash salt
1 tablespoon milk
1½ cups sifted confectioners' sugar
1 cup almond paste

Combine light corn syrup, vanilla, almond extract, and salt. Blend in milk. Add confectioners' sugar; mix well. Blend with almond paste. Shape mixture into round balls or, after tinting with appropriate food coloring, shape into miniature fruits. Makes about ¾ pound of candy.

NUT CREAMS

1 recipe BASIC UNCOOKED FONDANT
walnut or pecan halves

Prepare fondant as directed. Shape into ½-inch balls. Press each ball between 2 walnut or pecan halves. Makes about 1½ pounds of candy.

PEANUT SQUARES

⅓ cup butter
⅓ cup light corn syrup
1 teaspoon vanilla
½ teaspoon salt
1 pound confectioners' sugar, sifted
¾ cup coarsely chopped unsalted peanuts

Blend butter with the corn syrup, vanilla, and salt in a large mixing bowl. Add confectioners' sugar all at once and mix in, first with a spoon, then kneading with hands. Add chopped peanuts. Roll out or pat to ½-inch thickness. Cut into squares. Makes 1½ pounds of candy.

ALMOND DIAMONDS

⅓ *cup butter*
⅓ *cup light corn syrup*
1 *teaspoon almond extract*
½ *teaspoon salt*
1 *pound confectioners' sugar, sifted*
½ *cup coarsely chopped, toasted, blanched almonds*

Blend butter with the corn syrup, almond extract, and salt in a large mixing bowl. Add confectioners' sugar all at once and mix in, first with a spoon, then kneading with hands. Add almonds. Roll out or pat into ½-inch thickness. Cut into diamond shapes. Makes about 1½ pounds candy.

SALTED NUTS

1 *cup shelled nuts*
1 *tablespoon corn oil*
salt

Arrange nuts in a thin layer in a shallow baking pan. Pour corn oil over nuts; stir. Bake in 350°F. oven, stirring frequently, until nuts are lightly browned. Drain on absorbent paper. Sprinkle with salt. Makes 1 cup.

APRICOT NUT BALLS

3 *cups sugar*
1 *tablespoon instant tea powder*
½ *teaspoon salt*
1½ *cups dairy sour cream*
1 *cup chopped dried apricots*
1½ *cups finely chopped walnuts*
1 *teaspoon vanilla*

In a large saucepan, combine sugar, instant tea powder, salt, sour cream, and apricots. Cook over medium heat, stirring constantly, until sugar is dissolved and mixture begins to boil. Cook, stirring occasionally, to 236°F. on the candy thermometer, or until a small amount forms a soft ball in cold water. Let cool 10 minutes. Sir in ½ cup of the nuts and vanilla. Cool for 1 hour. Beat mixture for 1 minute. Refrigerate for 30 minutes. Form mixture into ¾-inch balls; roll in remaining nuts. Store covered in refrigerator. Makes 8 dozen nut balls.

ALMOND CANDY

¾ pound butter
2 cups sugar
1 cup cut-up almonds
½ cup finely chopped almonds
2 milk chocolate candy bars, 7½-ounce size

In a saucepan, combine butter, sugar, and cut-up almonds. Cook over low heat, stirring constantly, until the mixture reaches 310°F. on the candy thermometer, the hard crack stage. Don't let it scorch. Pour into a large buttered pan. Sprinkle finely chopped almonds over the surface. Press pieces of the chocolate bars on top of the hot candy; as they melt, spread the chocolate into a thin coating over the candy. Cool and break into pieces. Makes about 5 dozen pieces.

FROSTED NUTS

4 cups filberts, walnuts, or other nuts
2 egg whites
1 cup sugar
½ teaspoon cinnamon

Dip the nuts into unbeaten egg whites. Lift them out with a slotted spoon and roll them in sugar-cinnamon mixture. Spread the coated nuts in a shallow pan and bake in a 250°F. oven for 15 minutes, or until exteriors are crusty. Store in airtight container.

CHOCOLATE ORANGE WALNUT SQUARES

3 cups sugar
½ cup water
½ cup orange juice
2 cups semi-sweet chocolate chips
4 cups coarsely chopped walnuts
1 tablespoon grated orange rind

Line a 10 by 15-inch pan with aluminum foil. In a large heavy saucepan, combine sugar, water, and orange juice. Cook over high heat, stirring constantly. Boil for 3 minutes, until candy thermometer registers 230°F. Remove from heat and cool for 5 minutes. Add semi-sweet chocolate chips and stir until mixture is smooth. Quickly stir in walnuts and orange rind. Spread in the pan. Let cool and remove from pan. Cut into 1-inch squares. Makes about 12 dozen candies.

Cereal and
Popcorn Candies

For years popcorn and dried cereals have been the basis for impromptu refreshments from the pantry. With just a little more effort you can turn the same ingredients into cracker jacks and skrunch, if you cook a little syrup to bind the tender morsels together.

Don't overlook the wonderful possibilities of using home-made popcorn balls for holiday decorations. Use the Quick Candied Popcorn recipe in this chapter to make popcorn-gumdrop strings to decorate a real down-home Christmas tree. Shape the mixture into ¾-inch balls and, using a large needle and heavy nylon thread, string the balls alternately with large gumdrops. Drape over the evergreen branches to your heart's desire.

You can hang the popcorn balls individually if you wish by putting a loop of ribbon in the center of each popcorn ball before you form it. Leave a long loop hanging out of the top of the balls so you can hang them on the lower branches for all good little girls and boys—and maybe for a few naughty older ones too!

Make a novelty wreath to hang on the door by doubling the recipe and then shaping the mixture into a huge circle. While the mixture is still sticky, attach gilded pine cones and bows as the spirit moves you. Don't be surprised to find little chunks broken off as the door swings open and shut. Hungry hands have a way of reaching out for goodies, and even Santa might take a bit to nibble on during his long ride home.

Perhaps you will think of making an eye-opening centerpiece for a children's party by tinting the popcorn as directed in the last paragraph of the Candied Popcorn recipe. Pile the popcorn balls in a large bowl after they have dried, wrapping each ball with colored cellophane if you wish. Give one to each child when the party is over as part of the take-home loot.

Some children seem to have an endless sweet-tooth problem. Prepare cereal-based skrunch for them; this ought to ease your conscience somewhat. Tuck some skrunch into the lunch boxes to show that you have been thinking of them.

Here is an area of candymaking where you can really be inventive. Add raisins, dried fruits, and all kinds of nuts to create your own concoctions from these recipes—just take an old-fashioned method and bring it up-to-date by doing your own thing.

QUICK POPCORN BALLS

¼ cup corn oil
½ cup popcorn, unpopped
½ cup dark corn syrup
½ cup sugar
½ teaspoon salt

Heat corn oil in a 4-quart kettle over medium heat. Add popcorn. Cover, leaving a small air space at edge of cover. Shake frequently until popping stops. Meanwhile, mix together corn syrup, sugar, and salt; add to popped corn in the kettle and stir constantly over medium heat for 3 to 5 minutes, or until corn is evenly coated with mixture. Remove from heat. Grease hands, if desired. Form into balls, using as little pressure as possible. Makes 10 to 12 medium-sized popcorn balls.

PASTEL POPCORN BALLS

Follow the above recipe, substituting light corn syrup for dark corn syrup. To make pink popcorn balls, flavor syrup with 1 teaspoon oil of wintergreen and add 2 drops of red food coloring before stirring into popped corn. To make green popcorn balls, flavor syrup with 1 teaspoon oil of peppermint and add 2 drops of green food coloring before stirring into popped corn.

OLD-FASHIONED POPCORN BALLS

1 cup dark corn syrup
1 cup brown sugar
¼ cup water
1 teaspoon white vinegar
2 tablespoons butter
4 quarts unsalted popped corn
cinnamon

Mix together corn syrup, sugar, water, and vinegar in a saucepan. Bring to a boil over medium heat, stirring constantly. Continue cooking, stirring occasionally, until temperature reaches 260°F. on the candy thermometer (hard ball stage). Remove from heat. Quickly stir in butter. Sprinkle popcorn with cinnamon. Slowly pour over popped corn in a large bowl or pan, mixing well. Grease your hands well and shape into balls, using as little pressure as possible. Makes about 30 (2½-inch) balls.

CANDIED POPCORN

1 cup sugar
1 tablespoon butter
3 tablespoons water
3 quarts popped corn

In a saucepan, combine sugar, butter, and water; bring to a boil and cook until 220°F. on the candy thermometer, or when the mixture dropped off a spoon begins to "hair." Toss in popped corn and stir briskly until each kernel is coated. Remove from heat and stir until the mixture is cooled. Each grain should be separate and crystallized with candy. Makes 3 quarts.

Making popcorn at the Centennial Exposition, Philadelphia, 1876.

PEPPERMINT POPCORN

10 cups popped corn
⅔ cup pecans
⅓ cup toasted blanched almonds
⅔ cup light corn syrup
2 tablespoons water
1 pound confectioners' sugar, sifted
16 regular marshmallows
¾ teaspoon peppermint extract

Grease two jelly roll pans or large trays, and arrange popcorn and nuts in them. Combine corn syrup, water, and 1 cup confectioners' sugar in a medium saucepan; cook over low heat, stirring constantly, until sugar is dissolved. Gradually add remaining confectioners' sugar. Cook over low heat, stirring constantly, until mixture comes to a full boil. Add marshmallows; stir until melted. Remove from heat. Stir in peppermint extract. Pour mixture over popcorn and nuts. Toss until all is well coated. Let set at least 1 hour. Break apart into clusters. Makes about 3 quarts of candy.

CHOCOLATE COATED POPCORN

2 quarts salted popped corn
1 cup light corn syrup
1 cup sugar
½ cup water
2 tablespoons butter
2 squares unsweetened chocolate, 1-ounce size, melted

Put popped corn in a large bowl (large enough to hold twice the amount); set aside. Combine corn syrup, sugar, water, and butter in a saucepan. Cook over medium heat, stirring constantly, to 290°F. (hard crack stage). Remove from heat. Add melted chocolate; blend well. Slowly pour the hot mixture over the popped corn, stirring until the corn is uniformly covered. Turn coated corn onto a large pan or tray; separate the kernels of corn, working quickly, and spread on trays to cool. Makes about 2½ quarts popcorn.

CRACKER JACKS

2 quarts popped corn
2 cups shelled peanuts
1 cup molasses
½ cup sugar

Put the popped corn and the peanuts in a roasting pan, mixing them well. Combine the molasses and sugar in a deep heavy saucepan; cook until the syrup spins a thread when dropped into cold water, or the candy thermometer reaches 234°F. Pour hot mixture over the popped corn and peanuts, mixing well until all becomes cold and hard. Then break apart into chunks. Makes 2½ quarts of candy.

CARAMEL POPCORN

¼ cup corn oil
½ cup popcorn
1 cup salted peanuts or cashew nuts
1 cup dark corn syrup
1 cup sugar
¼ cup water
¼ cup butter

Grease two baking sheets. Heat oil in a 4-quart kettle over medium heat for 3 minutes. Add popcorn. Cover, leaving small air space at edge of cover. Shake frequently over medium heat until popping stops. Put popcorn into large greased heat-resistant bowl. Add nuts. Place mixture in a 300°F. oven until syrup is prepared.

Combine dark corn syrup, sugar, water, and butter in a heavy 2-quart saucepan. Stirring constantly, bring to a boil over medium heat. Continue cooking, stirring occasionally, until temperature reaches 280°F. on the candy thermometer (soft crack stage). Remove popcorn mixture from oven. Gradually pour syrup over mixture, stirring quickly until kernels are evenly coated. Spread mixture on baking sheets. Grease your hands and spread out into a thin layer. Cool. Separate into clusters. Store in a tightly covered container. Makes about 1½ pounds.

POPCORN ALMOND BRITTLE

1½ cups sugar
½ cup light corn syrup
½ cup water
½ teaspoon salt
4 cups prepared popcorn
1 cup slivered almonds
½ cup chopped candied cherries
2 tablespoons butter
1 teaspoon vanilla

Grease a shallow pan well. Combine sugar, corn syrup,

water, and salt in a heavy saucepan. Stir over low heat until sugar is dissolved. Cook over medium heat to 300°F. on the candy thermometer (hard crack stage). Meanwhile spread popcorn, nuts, and cherries in the shallow pan and heat in a 350°F. oven for 10 minutes. Remove syrup from heat; quickly stir in butter and vanilla; stir until butter melts. Pour over popcorn-almond mixture; toss. Spread mixture thin on a flat surface. Cool. Break into small pieces. Makes 1¼ pounds of candy.

POPCORN PEANUT BRITTLE

1½ cups sugar
½ cup dark corn syrup
½ cup water
½ teaspoon salt
4 cups prepared popcorn
1 cup shelled peanuts
2 tablespoons butter
1 teaspoon vanilla

Combine sugar, corn syrup, water, and salt in a heavy saucepan. Stir over low heat until sugar is dissolved. Cook over medium heat to 300°F. on the candy thermometer (hard crack stage). Meanwhile, spread popcorn and nuts in a well-greased shallow pan and heat in a 350°F. oven for 10 minutes. Remove syrup from heat; quickly stir in butter and vanilla; stir until butter melts. Pour over popcorn-nut mixture; toss. Spread mixture thin on a flat surface. Cool. Break into small pieces. Makes 1¼ pounds of candy.

MOLASSES POPCORN SQUARES

1 quart popped corn
1 cup sugar
¼ cup corn syrup
¼ cup water
2 tablespoons molasses
1 tablespoon butter or margarine
1 teaspoon salt

Butter a marble slab or platter. Discard all hard kernels in the popped corn; chop or grind the corn coarsely. In a saucepan, combine sugar, corn syrup, and water; cook and stir until it boils. Continue cooking until candy thermometer reaches 270°F. or until candy cracks when dropped into cold water. Add molasses and butter; cook to 290°F. or until it is very hard when dropped into cold water. Add chopped popcorn; stir well and return to heat for a moment to loosen. Immediately pour mixture onto the marble slab or platter. Roll thin with a rolling pin. Cut in squares or break into pieces if preferred. Makes about 1 quart of candy.

CHOCOLATE SKRUNCH

1 cup corn flakes
1 cup oven-toasted rice cereal
1 cup salted peanuts
1 cup broken nuts
¾ cup corn syrup
¼ cup sugar
2 tablespoons butter
2 cups semi-sweet chocolate chips
½ teaspoon vanilla extract

Line a 9-by-5-by-3-inch loaf pan with waxed paper. In a large bowl, combine corn flakes, rice cereal, peanuts, and broken nuts; set aside. In a large saucepan, combine corn syrup, sugar, and butter; bring to a boil over medium heat, stirring constantly. Boil for 2½ minutes. Remove from heat. Immediately stir in semi-sweet chocolate chips and vanilla. Quickly pour over cereal mixture and toss to coat evenly. Press into the loaf pan. Chill 2 hours until set. Cut into ½-inch slices and then cut each slice into four pieces. Makes about 1¾ pounds of candy.

PEANUT BUTTER SKRUNCH

2 cups corn flakes
2 cups crisp rice cereal
½ cup semi-sweet chocolate chips
¾ cup dark corn syrup
¼ cup sugar
2 tablespoons butter
½ cup chunk-style peanut butter
½ teaspoon almond extract

Combine corn flakes, rice cereal, and chocolate chips in a bowl; set aside. Mix corn syrup, sugar, and butter in a saucepan; bring to a boil over medium heat, stirring constantly. Boil for 3 minutes. Remove from heat. Cool for 10 minutes. Stir in peanut butter and almond extract. Beat mixture with a wooden spoon until it thickens. Pour over cereal mixture. Toss to coat evenly. Pack into a milk carton as directed in CARAMEL CHOCOLATE SKRUNCH. Makes about 1 pound.

PEANUT AND RAISIN SKRUNCH

2 cups corn flakes
1 cup crisp rice cereal
½ cup raisins
1 cup chopped peanuts
¾ cup dark corn syrup
¼ cup sugar
2 tablespoons butter
1 teaspoon cinnamon
½ teaspoon vanilla

Mix together corn flakes, rice cereal, raisins, and chopped peanuts; set aside. Mix corn syrup, sugar, butter, and cinnamon in a saucepan; bring to a boil over medium heat, stirring constantly. Boil for 3 minutes. Remove from heat. Cool for 10 minutes. Add vanilla. Beat mixture with a wooden spoon until mixture turns a light brown and thickens. Pour over cereal mixture. Toss to coat evenly. Pack into a milk carton as directed in CARAMEL CHOCOLATE SKRUNCH. Makes about 1 pound.

CARAMEL CHOCOLATE SKRUNCH

2 cups corn flakes
1 cup crisp rice cereal
½ cup semi-sweet chocolate chips
1 cup broken nuts
¾ cup dark corn syrup
¼ cup sugar
2 tablespoons butter
½ teaspoon vanilla

Cut top off of a 1-quart milk carton. Mix together corn flakes, rice cereal, chocolate chips, and nuts in a bowl; set aside. Mix corn syrup, sugar, and butter in a saucepan; bring to a boil over medium heat, stirring constantly. Boil for 3 minutes. Remove from heat. Cool for 10 minutes. Add vanilla. Beat mixture with wooden spoon until mixture turns a light brown and thickens. Pour over cereal mixture. Toss to coat evenly. Pack firmly into the milk carton. Chill until set—1 or 2 hours. Cut off end of carton and down one side with a sharp knife. Peel off carton. Cut candy into slices. Refrigeration is not required after loaf is set. Makes about 1 pound.

NOTE: To make free-form shapes, do not press mixture into the carton. Cool about 15 minutes and then shape as desired.

Caramel chocolate skrunch.

Index

1 2 3 4 5 6 7 ← P Y → 9 8 7 6 5 4